I believe that the true currency of business is relationships. This book is an invaluable gift, full of ways you can launch a business and build relationships with people. Download it, read it, but most importantly, do it!

—Matt Bird, CEO of Relationology Ltd.,
and author of *Relationology 101*

Working from home is fine if you have a job, but what if you don't? To the rescue comes Jim Palumbo with his pithy book. All you need is passion, perseverance, and a connection to the Internet. This is a wonderful resource for those who are newly unemployed or bored with retirement and seeking extra income, or who just want to take control of their financial lives.

—Dan Solin, *New York Times* best-selling author
of the Smartest series of books

START YOUR DREAM BUSINESS TODAY

101 BUSINESSES YOU CAN START WITH NO MONEY OR EDUCATION

JAMES G. PALUMBO

MEDIA

MEDIA

Published 2022 by Gildan Media LLC
aka G&D Media
www.GandDmedia.com

Front Cover design by David Rheinhardt of Pyrographx

Interior design by Meghan Day Healey of Story Horse, LLC

Library of Congress Cataloging-in-Publication Data is available upon request

ISBN: 978-1-7225-0573-8

10   9   8   7   6   5   4   3   2   1

Contents

Preface

A pessimist sees the difficulty in every opportunity;
an optimist sees opportunity in every difficulty.
—WINSTON CHURCHILL

The coronavirus pandemic has awakened the whole world to the freedom and magic of the work-from-home environment, which has blessed my family and me for nearly two decades.

My wife, Cheri, and I sold the first two businesses we started and decided to move to an island off the Gulf Coast. I had been migrating my investment advisory practice to the Internet for a while and believed I could use Internet tools to work from a home office. The island was ninety miles from my former office, so it would require a change of day-to-day practices to make the transition. I switched from paper to digital reports and files, outsourced administration, and introduced video conferencing. I not only made the transition work but grew the business ten times while working from home under a patio umbrella.

A typical day started by putting on a ball cap to keep the sun out of my eyes while I was looking at the laptop screen, filling a mug of coffee, propping my feet up on the railing of the deck, and watching the boats exit the marina as I fired up the computer to begin my workday. Cheri might bring me a coffee refill, or I might jump in the pool for a couple of laps between teleconferences.

Eventually my company merged with our professional services outsourcer, Dynamic Advisor Solutions. Today Dynamic provides professional services to dozens of advisory practices around the United States and has billions in assets under administration, all from a 100 percent cloud-based platform. (To learn more about the cloud, see the Glossary at the end of this book.) Our entire staff works remotely from locations on three continents.

Working remotely has not only facilitated the healthy growth of our business, it has enabled our employees to reclaim the time that was wasted on commuting, allowed them to spend that time with their families, and provided the flexibility for them to pursue personal and professional growth. In fact, 52 percent of small businesses in America are home-based. A cloud-based virtual environment and platform, combined with a remote workforce, has fueled such incredible cost and operational efficiency that Dynamic now serves as a cutting-edge model for wealth advice in the twenty-first century.

One of the true differentiating factors in this book is the unique approach I take in the previously undefined theological and philosophical model of Biblenomics™. This concept is interwoven throughout the chapters, principles, and illustrations I'll be presenting. Biblenomics is a conceptual part of the Eternal Decree, which is based on Ephesians 1:11: "In Him also we have obtained an inheritance, being predestined according to the purpose of Him who works all things according to the counsel of His will."[1] The Eternal Decree says that God controls all events in His creation. Biblenom-

---

1 Biblical quotations are from the New King James Version.

ics is also an applied philosophy that has guided me throughout my ministry and successful business endeavors.

Biblenomics is God's system of economics. It forms the bedrock ideology of success embedded in this work, not by me, but by the Author of life and stewardship. I believe that the Reformation is the foundation of Western civilization, which, with its free markets, property rights, and sanctity of contract, is a direct expression of God's plan for us through the societies born from the Reformation. The twenty-first-century system of trade, economics, and business is the practical testimony of God's plan for man, the fruit of the Reformers' and Puritans' work ethic and moral absolutes. In the pursuit of financial security for our family through our business, we bring empathy into our community and into our neighbor's lives. Thereby the invisible hand of God is seen by all, superintending the most prosperous global economy in the history of mankind, just as Adam Smith predicted in his 1776 book *The Wealth of Nations*.

Biblenomics is more than random principles or lessons taken from isolated Bible stories, verses, or proof texts. It is God's expression of Himself and His purpose for mankind, found in the holistic way He teaches us to steward our earthly wealth, possessions, and family.

Jesus's teachings show us, with childlike simplicity, how to live out divine love in our workaday lives through our words, actions, tools, and earthly possessions. In the twenty-first century, money is the proxy for all these earthly possessions. Our handling of money, work, and business is where the rubber meets the road when it comes to living our life the way that God intended.

My dear friends, this is the ridiculously simple path to the beautiful life for which we all long: to live our life honoring God, loving others completely and selflessly, and letting our business be an expression of that beautiful life.

Biblenomics recognizes God's decree, which outlines His plan and purpose for the world and for us individually. It acknowledges that everything that happens in the world and in our lives has a purpose, even though we don't know what it may be ahead of time, and that under this grand purpose of sovereign God we can live a life *coram Deo* (a Latin phrase meaning *in the presence of God*). We live a life of wholeness under the superintending hand and authority of God, all to His honor. In no clearer way is this expressed than when you wake up Monday morning and execute your business plan according to the principles of Biblenomics under the superintending providence of the invisible hand of God.

I'm sharing my story, and the things that God has taught me in life, to inspire you to succeed: to affirm that you can start a business from nothing and grow it into a multimillion-dollar enterprise. Being a contrarian in today's world—doing the right thing, serving a higher purpose, and working remotely—is not necessarily a barrier to your success but may be the launchpad for fulfilling your dreams and aspirations.

Introduction

The secret of getting ahead is getting started.
—MARK TWAIN

Let's go! Pick up your head, get out of the chair, and just do something. It doesn't matter what you do, so long as it ain't nothin'. You've been dreaming; now start doing.

In the journey of life, there are dreamers, there are doers, and then there are dreamers that do. I want you to be someone that has a dream who does something with it. There are few greater regrets in life than to have a vision of your future without ever even trying to achieve it. "Many people die with their music still in them. Too often it is because they are always getting ready to live. Before they know it, time runs out," wrote Oliver Wendell Holmes.

Making money is easy! It's as easy as picking apples from a tree, but you can't do it sitting on the sofa. You need to stand up, walk out the door, and use your new business to harvest the money that is waiting for you. Money is readily available: it has velocity, it is in motion, and it is easy to earn. The pie is getting larger in these unprecedented times of growth and global economic expansion. Perhaps most important to remember is *people are desperately trying to give it to you.* They really are.

People are desperately trying to give you money.

I say making money is easy because the opportunities are within your grasp. There is no mystery or secret to achieving success. Ordinary people can succeed by ordinary means, without significant capital or advanced education. This does not imply that success comes without hard work. In fact, I can promise you that you will work harder as an entrepreneur than you have ever worked before. Success in life requires that you put in the work.

Opportunity is missed by most people because it is dressed in overalls and looks like work.   —Thomas Edison

Van Gogh's master teacher told him, "'I am glad you have to paint on an empty stomach; nothing in this world, worthwhile had ever been achieved comfortably . . . and nothing worthwhile that we have to give is due to a comfortable habit." To this, I add: lean into your discomfort, move out of your comfort zone, work hard, and you will eventually achieve success.

What is going to stop you from achieving your goal? Is it *the Man?* Is it *the System?* Is it your skin color, nationality, or your current financial condition? No: these may be challenges and obstacles, but you can overcome them; I know you can. The only thing that can kill your dreams is you—nobody else. Your destiny is determined by you and Providence. You've dreamed about starting a business; now let's take action and do it!

Providence is not merely God's plan, which is optional for us to realize. It is the superintending hand of God at work in our lives, steering us to the purpose He has destined for us. To say, "Your destiny is determined by you and Providence," implies profound existential and metaphysical truths: that life is a combination of self-actualization and the invisible hand of God at work, guiding, nudging, and ordaining circumstances to bring us to our best. We can't control that part—it's on God. The daily diligence and the Golden Rule part is on us.

Do the Right Thing

When you start your business with the sole purpose of helping others, you will succeed. If you choose to cultivate vitality, integrity, generosity, honesty, and diligence in your own character, your business will reflect the kind of man or woman you have chosen to be. If you live by the Golden Rule, caring more about others than yourself, pursue excellence, sincerely strive to help people, and display honesty in all things, you are destined to reap what you have sown. Plant good works, and you will harvest good fruits. These are the foundation stones upon which every good business is built.

Your Biggest Obstacles

Your biggest obstacles are personal vices and lack of character—things like imbibing too much alcohol or lack of diligence. These vices and flaws will prevent those customers *who want to buy from you* from giving you money. They are out there, money in hand, waiting for you to show up and do the right thing! But they need to trust in who you are and what you stand for.

Make the right choice, and build up your character as your first step. Personal development is the beginning of the journey to success. Use this business startup as a catalyst for your personal and professional growth. *Not every business you start will succeed, but every person can succeed in business.* Just persevere and begin with integrity.

Mastery: the desire to get better and better at something that matters.

Purpose: the yearning to do what we do in the service of something larger than ourselves.

These are the building blocks of an entirely new operation system for our businesses.

—Daniel Pink, author of *When* and *Drive*

I used to pass by a small coffee shop each day while driving the kids to and from school. I noticed that the business was closed when I drove by at 7:00 a.m. but open when I picked the kiddos up at 3:00 p.m., with cars in the parking lot, implying that people liked the product. So where was the owner in the morning? As I imagined the potential surrounding this small business, I thought, "What an irony! Here is a barista who cannot wake themselves up in the morning to make the coffee!"

Poor personal habits and shallowness of character will sink your business faster than anything else.

Of course, the "I'm not a morning person" coffee shop is now shuttered, and a new business has moved into its space. If you serve tasty coffee and pastries, you can make money in almost any city in the world—but not if you can't to get yourself up and open your business for the morning coffee crowd!

It is highly probable that the main ingredients to your success are not things like the sophistication of your business plan or your ability to obtain a Small Business Administration (SBA) loan. Rather, your success depends on the little things, like whether you can turn off the television, go to bed early, wake up in the morning, and go make a killing in your business.

It's Easy to Sell but Hard to Buy

Selling your product or service is *sooo* easy. Being a consumer is the tougher job. Many businesses are woefully lacking in basic communication skills, customer service, etiquette, and courtesy. Think about the times you have gone into a business looking for a product, or the times you called a business with a few questions, intending to buy products or services. But you just couldn't find the product you wanted or were unable to obtain answers to your questions. Too many merchants are so disorganized and distracted that you can't give them your money, no matter how hard you try!

You will occasionally find me in my office yelling at my phone—and no, there is no one on the other end of the call. Why am I yelling? Because I just made a phone call, the most important business call that every entrepreneur would like to receive: *"I'm calling to give you my money."* You would think that this would elicit dancing and celebration at the business I am calling, but often, to my surprise, the person at the business does not answer the phone, does not call me back promptly, or worst of all, sounds annoyed that I have interrupted their lunch.

In order to succeed, you must do the opposite of these businesses. Create a great customer experience. Give people what they want, when they want it, and do the right thing always, everywhere, and to everyone. Conduct yourself with integrity, joy, and enthusiasm, and genuinely care about others, and you will build a great business.

Getting Started

If you want to be a successful entrepreneur, you need to start with these two simple, foundational principles:

1. **Give people what they want.** Find out what people want, and give it to them.
2. **Do the right thing.** Always, everywhere, and to everyone.

Find Out What People Want

When asked the secret of his success, Starbucks founder Howard Shultz responded, "Simple. Find out what people want, and give it to them." People wanted a comfortable place to enjoy good coffee, and Shultz gave it to them.

Don't sell just what you personally like; make sure your business meets a need, giving people what they want. I met several bored housewives who were drinking too much wine. Thinking themselves experts on wine, they spent hundreds of thousands of dollars to open wine bars, only to lose all their money on the venture. Drinking wine does not make you an expert on wine or imply that people will come to your wine bar. Instead, find out what people really want in your community.

In her book *Effectuation: Elements of Entrepreneurial Expertise,* Saras Sarasvathy describes the *pilot-in-the-plane principle,* meaning that the future is something you change by your actions. In other words, you can create your own opportunities and demand. Sarasvathy's principles include the *bird-in-hand,* where you create solutions with the resources you have in hand now, and the *lemonade* principle, which acknowledges that mistakes and surprises can be exploited to create new opportunities.

Yes, you can start a business where there is no apparent need or demand; you can create or uncover the demand. I didn't know I needed Wi-Fi on a plane or a GPS in my watch, but once I discovered them, I couldn't live without them. Such businesses may take a long time and may require massive amounts of seed capital to create a new market. I'm not arguing against this type of innovation—it's driving the global economy in the twenty-first century. But for our purposes in this book, we'll be exploring simpler, meet-the-demand or give-people-what-they-want opportunities that you can start with little cash or special training.

Always Do the Right Thing

No matter what the cost or how much you will be personally inconvenienced, you've got to do the right thing—always, everywhere, and to everyone. Honesty and integrity are more important than earning money. We honor God when we conduct our business by the Book, putting people and ethics ahead of greed and profits. If you do the right thing, put people first, meet their needs, help them, and always remember that you are a steward of the resources with which God has entrusted you, you will always be successful. There are numerous examples of people doing the right thing as a way of life, not just as a business technique:

- Madam C. J. Walker was the first self-made female African American millionaire in America. After she started her own hair care line, wannabe entrepreneurs asked her the secret to her success from poverty to riches. She would tell them that faith in God, quality products, and "honest business dealings" fueled her ascent.

- James Cash Penney, founder of the J. C. Penney chain, was the son of a Baptist minister and a 33rd-degree Freemason who gave much of his time and money to charity. He originally called his shop The Golden Rule Store, believing that the secret to success was treating others the way they wanted to be treated.
- Sam Walton worked as a clerk at a J. C. Penney store until he opened the first Walmart, continuing to build on the Golden Rule. Walmart has grown to more than 10,000 stores employing over 2 million people.
- Dave Thomas, founder of the Wendy's burger chain, was an orphan. He formed the Dave Thomas Foundation for Adoption to find "forever homes for children in foster care." Dave never knew his birth mother. His adoptive mother died when he was five years old, and he lost two stepmothers before he was the age of ten. Wendy's grew to 1,000 restaurants in less than ten years based on Dave's hardworking, "mop-bucket attitude."

I could go on for pages giving you examples of men and women who chose to do the right thing, built successful businesses on an ethical foundation, and today are making a difference in the world through their charities and foundations. They didn't start with greed; they built on the precept of do the right thing. Don't wait until you get rich to serve—start today, and it will fuel your success.

Differentiation

It's been said that there are no new ideas, simply different ways of approaching customers, providing a service, or making a product. The key here is to differentiate yourself from others who are doing similar work.

There is no such thing as a new idea. It is impossible. We simply take a lot of old ideas and put them into a sort of mental kaleidoscope. We give them a turn and they make new and curious combinations. We keep on turning and making new combinations indefinitely; but they are the same old pieces of colored glass that have been in use through all the ages. —Mark Twain

What makes your business different from others in the same space? If you are in a food business, do you offer something that most others do not? How about a vegan food truck? I'm not saying there aren't *any*, but there aren't *many*. Another example: if you were raised Fijian or Afghan, you may have knowledge of a cuisine that is not common in many areas.

What's your differentiator? Be careful starting a business that everyone is in. There are plenty of cell phone repair places, but how many mobile repair persons? There are a few, but not many. Check out FiXiT.com. It's a great idea, but there are forty-seven states that *don't* have a FiXiT Mobile Repair service provider. Do your research, and you will find opportunities to fill a need in your community, rather than doing the same thing everyone else is doing.

In order to be irreplaceable, one must always be *different*.

—Coco Chanel

What differentiators can you think of related to your business idea? Jot them down—and don't self-edit.

The X-Factor

For many, the X-factor refers to your differentiator, but I want it to mean much more to you. In addition to differentiation, I want you to think about your spiritual or emotional connection with your clients. By my definition, the difference between a differentiator and the X-factor is the *emotional* or *spiritual* connection.

My friends who are in fair trade businesses sell products that are not necessarily uncommon, but they are produced by people who are paid fairly, and to whom the distributor or entrepreneur is teaching the dignity of financial independence under improved environmental and social standards. Their story resonates with many customers who will purchase goods at a higher price in order to support the business's fair trade mission. This is an X-factor. It is a differentiator: it makes an emotional or spiritual connection with the customer. Here's one of my favorite examples.

There is an episode of *Shark Tank* featuring Combat Flip Flops, whose aim is, according to its website, to "make cool stuff in dangerous places." Founder Matthew Griffin's values revolve around persistence, creativity, and respect. His TED talk reveals his compassion for the people of Afghanistan. His X-factor is in his mantra: "Business, not bullets: Grow entrepreneurs in conflict areas. Build communities and fund women's education." In Afghanistan, only 15 percent of women are literate—but his company has a women-run factory there. His motto: "Manufacture peace through trade. The Unarmed Forces." Griffin's story was so compelling that billionaire entrepreneur Mark Cuban brushed aside the other sharks' questions about cost and sales, and said, "The cost doesn't matter; I'm in." Cuban believed so strongly in the spiritual mission of the business that nothing could stop him from investing. In the end, all five sharks invested in Combat Flip Flops. They are an example of a powerful X-factor. It goes beyond simply product differentiation and connects with your customer emotionally and spiritually. They can't help but buy from you.

An X-factor in business is the ability to add intangible value to your product or service. —Tony Robbins

---

When my wife was running a women's-only fitness club, part of the membership sales process was to ask the prospective member why she was considering joining the club. She usually answered that she wanted to lose weight or tone up. Then the membership associate would ask, "Yes, I understand, but what is the reason you want to lose weight? What is motivating you?"

Often the customer's eyes would fill with tears, and she would reveal the emotional pain she was suffering as a result of her obesity: "My husband won't touch me." Or, "I haven't had a date in two years."

Suddenly the associate had discovered the X-factor, the deep-down motivation for considering the fitness club's service. The value relationship between the club and the client had now changed from "Give me the shortest membership at the lowest price" to a life-changing and transformative spiritual and physical journey that staff and client would take together. The results for many of these women transcended mere exercise. They uncovered their inner discipline, rediscovered their personal intrinsic value, regained their confidence, and revived their relationships.

Discovering the X-factor in your business will help you deliver more value to your clients, create loyal customers that never leave, and help you be more successful.

Fatally Unique

I've encouraged you to be different and find your differentiator and X-factor, but I don't want you to be fatally unique. You can be so out of the ordinary that your business is just weird (there is good weird and bad weird; you don't want to be bad weird), out of the demand zone, or incomprehensible to clients. I met a hopeful entrepreneur who wanted to open a wine bar bookstore. (Why do so many business ideas include wine?) The idea of people sitting in sofas drinking wine and reading books was very appealing to her aesthetic sense and her emotions, but it was a flawed idea that would attract little clientele. Some research would reveal that book sales are migrating to online resellers at lightning speed and that people prefer food with their wine. The business died of fatal uniqueness. Another acquaintance started a combined wine bar and furniture store, uncovering her fatal uniqueness, but quickly pivoted to food and wine and now runs one of the most popular restaurants in McAllen, Texas, called House Wine.

There is a thin line between being creative and being fatally unique. If commerce is a river, then you need to stay on the left or right of the mainstream of demand. Mainstream demand is midcurrent in the river of commerce. It is where consumers desire goods and services. However, it may be difficult for you, as a new or small business, to compete with large volume sellers of mainstream brands. For example, your e-store would have difficulty competing with Sam's Club or Wayfair in the patio furniture marketplace, but you may be able to make a killing with unusual imports or handmade artisan patio furniture. You're now competing in a high-demand market, but not for the high-volume, low-cost mainstream customers.

In his book *The Long Tail: Why the Future of Business Is Selling Less of More*, Chris Anderson argues that consumers are seeking a more curated buying experience and doing more niche or artisan buying. Anderson has a theory he calls *the long tail concept*, according to which less popular goods can actually increase profitability as consumers have begun navigating away from mainstream markets and looking for that nichey or artisan buying experience. If you can't compete with the high-volume competitors, then sell hard-to-find items at higher prices. Just be careful to not go so far outside of the mainstream that you are fatally unique.

The motto "Find out what people want, and give it to them" is still your guidepost. It is difficult to create a new market. If you are patient and blessed, you can invent or create demand for a product that doesn't exist yet, but those wins are few and far between. I don't want to discourage you from pursuing your dreams. Go for it if you feel this is your calling. I'll be cheering for you. For this book, however, I want to focus on consistent wins in small business start-ups, by providing 101 no-brainer ideas that you can ramp up quickly with little to no money or special training. Some ideas in this book capitalize on a talent you may already have, such as woodworking or graphic art, so not all of them are for everyone, but they can inspire everyone to succeed in their own universe of unique characteristics, personality traits, and talent.

Stay on either side of the fast, deep water in the midcurrent of the river of commerce, and look for your tributary, eddy, or predictably manageable seam on either side of the tumult to start your business. Don't compete with big competitors in the middle of the stream, and don't be so unique you're up on the bank and out of the river. Find that spot that is uniquely you! You'll learn throughout these pages that mastering your individuality, uniqueness, specialization, and niche characterize the most successful businesses.

As I'm writing about mastering your individuality and uniqueness, I'm thinking about Palmer Luckey, who revived the virtual reality industry with his Oculus Rift, built in his mom's basement, which was acquired by Facebook for $3 billion. He was ultimately fired from Facebook because it was discovered that he supported a political candidate that reflected his personal worldview. Getting fired was a blessing in disguise. Facebook paid him $100 million for the wrongful termination, and shortly after he started an AI (artificial intelligence) company, Anduril.com, that is selling completely autonomous small unmanned aircraft systems (sUAS) or drones, called Ghosts, which operate in swarms without the need for human operators. They are used for security on large perimeters. Threat detection is transmitted to human agents in real time. Luckey builds things that are cooler than the sci-fi tech in movies, is earning hundreds of millions of dollars, and is building his own company—all because he chose to be himself.

Outline for Success

The business ideas that you read about in this book will include a narrative description and one or more of the following elements:

- Real-life success stories
- How to get started
- Marketing advice
- Tips and techniques for building your business
- Suggestions for horizontal growth
- Suggestions for vertical growth
- Variations

In addition, I've added a mini–business plan at the end of this book to help you start thinking concretely about making your idea come to life.

Real Life Success Stories

Each group of business ideas that you will read about comes from the story of a real person who has actually started and succeeded in the business you are reading about. What you are getting here are real case studies of real people and businesses, not hypothetical rubbish from a keyboard jockey or professor who never dirtied their hands or had to pay the bills with the income they created as an entrepreneur. This is real life, real people, real businesses, and real money. By the time I finished the research for this book, I found that these stories of toil and triumph, perseverance and prosperity have become my favorite parts of the book.

How to Get Started

The hardest part of getting started is getting started! The stories I've included provide inspiration as well as practical tips on what to do to get your business off the ground and take those important first steps.

Marketing

Products and services don't just sell themselves, particularly if your potential customers or clients can't find you. Many of the entrepreneurs I interviewed have shared their marketing tips, which often built their businesses from mere ideas to thriving enterprises that offer them lifestyles of financial security and freedom. Great marketing often equals a great business.

Tips and Techniques for Building Your Business

These are important practices that experienced entrepreneurs have learned through time, trial, and error. By sharing them here, I hope to save you time, effort, and money and put you on a fast track to success.

Vertical and Horizontal Growth

These two elements will help you expand your small business into an enterprise business, and ultimately into a large business. It is important to know the difference between *vertical growth* and *horizontal growth*. For example, a company that sells tacos to consumers would pursue horizontal growth by finding new distribution locations for their tacos and releasing new flavors and combos. By contrast, a company that is pursuing vertical growth is looking to expand to different points in the supply chain, such as manufacturing tortillas or developing a mobile app with which people can order their tacos to be delivered to their door.

Variations

Each idea represents one or more specific businesses I have observed or studied. For most of them, there is another, similar business that follows the same model but may sell a different product or service or utilize a different technique. These businesses are substantially similar, but are variations of the same successful theme, product, or process. For example, in the chapter on businesses employing trucks, trailers, and carts, there are tons of examples of profitable snow cone or shaved ice businesses. I have also added several other real-life examples of food and coffee sold from trucks, trailers, and carts. They are very similar, and the formula for success is almost the same for all. Some of these, like Josh and John's Scoop Bus, emerged from brick-and-mortar stores. This company has a bus that people can reserve for birthday parties, weddings, employee picnics, and similar occasions.

These are all variations on a theme—trucks, trailers, and carts are great fast-start options from which to sell many products. The numerous variations are substantially similar in many ways.

This brings us to our list of businesses. I promised you 101 business ideas, but you'll notice there are many more. That's because of these variation businesses. Some are variations on one or more categories. Just enjoy the journey exploring the myriad ideas that may spark your fire!

Stepping-Stone Businesses

Many of the businesses I will show you are stepping-stones to the business you ultimately want to be in. Cutting grass is not the career you want for the long term, but it may be a stepping-stone to running a five-star landscaping company or arborist business. Be patient and see it for what it is—a path to your dream business. You have to be willing to mop a lot of floors before you can be a CEO.

In the next chapter, you'll meet a man who went from being over $38,000 in debt to being debt-free in just three months. At this writing, eleven years later, Peach Hardy and his wife, Danielle, own businesses worth $1.3 million. How did he get there? He began with painting a deck for $250, and from there, the next right step appeared. Sometimes you have to step out on the first stepping-stone to discover what the next one will be. It's not always a straight line with visibility into the future, but I believe that once you start the journey, you will uncover multiple opportunities to grow in the direction of your dreams.

Analysis Paralysis

Avoid the trap of overplanning. It's good to be organized and have a plan, but be careful not to get stuck in the planning process. I know a boatload of hopeful entrepreneurs who have been refining their business plans for years, tinkering with legal and entity planning, setting up books, and hiring consultants, only to never sell a darn thing. I know a woman who had a dream of launching her own line of hair products. They were good products too! She spent years writing and revising her plan and producing sample products, but never sold a single container of product to anyone. You've got to start somewhere; don't overthink it.

Most successful entrepreneurs I know started their businesses with an idea, hard work, and delivering a great experience to customers. They leaped at the opportunity and then grew into their success. Ready, fire, aim! Just keep doing the right thing, and you will mature into your thriving business. Local community colleges and business development centers offer help to people wanting to start a business. They are a great resource; just don't get lost in the planning and consulting process. Put your plan together, and get to it right away.

You've got dreams and aspirations buried inside you; now it's time to bring them alive. You have the potential and power to do this, all you have to do is put one foot in front of the other; take the first steps on the journey to your destiny. Once you're moving forward, you'll be well on your way to the freedom and dignity of financial independence.

1
Why Be an Entrepreneur?

The best way to predict the future is to create it.
—PETER DRUCKER

There are many reasons why entrepreneurs go into business for themselves, but I believe that we all share a few in common.

Priorities and balance. Bring balance and ease to your life. You set your schedule and priorities. When you're able to put your faith and family first without having to serve your employer's priorities, you will have a sense of freedom unlike any other.

Being the CEO of YOU. Be the boss of you!

Build your dream, not your boss's dream. If you are going to give your hours, toil, sweat, and tears to your work, why not build your dream instead of someone else's? Why wind up at the end of your life with regrets about what you were inspired to do but didn't?

Building confidence. Overcome self-criticism, negative mindset, and unproductive behavior patterns. Each tiny success along the entrepreneurial path builds self-confidence.

Freedom. You get to choose what you do and when you do it 99 percent of the time!

Self-determination. Be the captain of your own future.

Living your dream. As Henry David Thoreau wrote, "Go confidently in the direction of your dreams. Live the life you've imagined. As you simplify your life, the laws of the universe will be simpler."

Unlimited income potential. You are limited only by your faith, inspiration, and perseverance.

The three best decisions I've made in my life were to commit my life to God, marry Cheri, and be an entrepreneur. Not surprisingly, they are all related. Being self-employed has enabled me to dedicate my life to my family and to the service of others while assigning work and business their rightful place on the list of life's priorities. Instead of being a slave to the fear of losing a paycheck, I took charge of my finances by being the captain of my own ship.

So where should work and business rank on the hierarchy of priorities? Surprisingly, it is solidly number four. It should always come behind our commitment to the things that matter most. Money is not the goal in life; rather it is a tool to help us help others.

Here in a nutshell is an eternal, unchangeable hierarchy of life's priorities. It is the encapsulation of all life's philosophy and legitimate worldviews; it is, in a nutshell, what the Bible teaches:

1. God
2. Family
3. Others
4. Stewardship

Numbers two and three are really the same. We should love everyone, everywhere, all the time, but I think there is a practical distinction here, because we have a special commitment to our families. Our families are the training ground for us. It is where we learn to perfect our serve and learn to love.

Executive summaries are great because they give you the Cliff Notes version of big ideas and subjects. Jesus summarized the entire history of philosophy, all religious life and teaching, the contents of the entire Bible, and our purpose in life into two sentences. He said (and I'm paraphrasing), "All of the moral law and the teachings of the words of the prophets are fulfilled in two commandments: to love God with all of your heart and mind and soul and strength and to love others as yourself" (Mark 12:29–31).

These words express the meaning and purpose of life with perfect clarity. With childlike simplicity, they tell us where our priorities should be. No equivocation, no compromise—this is our truth, and we've got to live it.

So what do we do with this whole prosperity, money, and success philosophy? We hear it everywhere: Do what you love. Pursue your passion. Find your fulfillment, meaning, and purpose in financial, career, and business success. I say, turn it upside down! Let me explain.

Jesus seems to spend an inordinate amount of time talking about money and business, such as in the parables of the talents, the unjust steward, and the workers in the vineyard. So what's the message? Is it love or is it money? I believe the answer is hidden in plain sight.

Your destiny in life is to love others, so you can't find your purpose and meaning in life through monetary success alone. It is only a tool to serve and love others. If you want to be a great businessperson, commit yourself to be a servant to your employees, helping all of them find success. Only by helping others succeed do we succeed ourselves. Success with money is important, not for its own sake but for the sake of others.

Only by helping others succeed do we succeed ourselves.

Why am I an entrepreneur? It's simple: because it gives me the freedom and wealth to serve others. That's it, my friend. No more, no less. If you get your priorities straight, you will not be driven by greed or ego, and you will be a rock star in business. You will be fulfilling your purpose in life. Free from the shackles of avarice, vice, and lucre, you can launch and grow your business quickly and successfully.

2
Career Pathing and Stepping-Stones

Find out what you like doing best and
get someone to pay you for doing it.
—KATHERINE WHITEHORN, JOURNALIST AND AUTHOR

"Hey, Jim! Come over here. I want you to meet somebody," said Pete Gatto. We were standing in front of the coffee bar at church. I had met Pete and his wife, Cheryl, an award-winning author, after moving to Colorado Springs. They also had just arrived in Colorado after several years running a youth camp in La Paz, Mexico. Pete is a great networker and loves to bring people together.

"This is Peach," said Pete. I couldn't miss the young man standing before me. Lean and outgoing, with asymmetrical tangerine hair, Peach shook my hand, and we began to talk about business. I was fascinated by his story. After hitting rock bottom in a life of music and drugs, he committed his life to God and submitted to doing what was right—exemplifying hard work, good stewardship, and a deep commitment to helping second-chancers start a new life. Not only was he blessed with business success, but he used his success to help others. The more he and his wife, Danielle, helped others, the more they prospered.

Following are excerpts from a recent discussion with Peach, where he tells part of his story. After that, I'll profile one of his businesses—a hair studio and the career path, plus outline an entrepreneurial path that it can represent for you.

Later in the book, I'll profile two additional businesses started by Peach and Danielle and the opportunities that they have pioneered, one of which might be a viable choice for you!

According to Peach

I asked Peach to tell us their story. How did he and Danielle become millionaires in just ten years?

"On March 10, 2008, I started IAAO, LLC, a management company for my band. I was the drummer, and music was the only place I felt competent, particularly playing the drums. I started when I was six years old. The company had a half-million-dollar overhead, with a tiny 2 percent profit margin. It only made $10,000 a year net, which had to be split between all the people on the road.

"That experience taught me how to manage a profit and loss statement. Even though there was a lot of money, I had to learn to spend wisely and steward really well. But no matter how hard I studied business and how hard we worked, the unexpected happened, and the band's bus broke down in Vero Beach, Florida. We had to end the tour early."

The result: Peach found himself $38,238 in debt.

"I will never forget that number," he says. "My wife and I were left with all the debt. The other band members were not willing to help us out of the hole. I was newly married, and I had to take responsibility. I couldn't just leave my new wife stranded. At the time, she was cutting hair at another salon and making $40,000 a year. It clearly would have been irresponsible."

So Peach did what he knew to do: he got down on his knees and prayed: "Lord, I am $38,238 in debt, and I need your help." He chuckles that he spoke the exact amount to God. He was very aware of the burden on him.

"The answer came quickly. It wasn't audible, but it was very clear: 'Whatever I put in your hands to do, do it well.' It just rang in my heart. About five minutes later, the phone rang. It was a friend of mine, who said, 'I have a deck you can paint. I'll pay you $250.' I ended the call and threw my phone to the ground, saying out loud, 'God, this isn't going to work!'

"I knew I had to be obedient, yet I was doing the math in my head, and not seeing how this was going to work. I would earn less than minimum wage, but I figured I just had to start and get my work ethic moving."

As Peach was painting the spindles of the deck, another friend strolled by and said, "That looks really good. I have a patio you can paint. I'll pay you $800." From there, Peach picked up other deck and repair jobs. Within three months, that debt was gone.

"What stops us so often is our own disobedience to God's plan," says Peach. "I can't imagine what our life would look like if I hadn't taken that first deck job. The $800 deck was easy. The $250 deck job was the hard one."

Within three months, Peach and Danielle were debt-free. All $38,238 had been paid off. Peach says, "If you can show people your vision, people will take a risk on you if they can see it." His friends took a risk on him, and it paid off well.

"Today," he continues, "my wife and I have a holding company that is worth $1.1 million, and investors are stepping in because I've shared my vision. We were thousands of dollars in debt, and now we own four different operations, all of which began with a vision."

Peach's willingness to ask God for help and obey the commands given to him factored into this success, not only in the beginning but throughout his career path.

After the debt was repaid, Peach was looking to do more than paint and repair decks. In 2010, he and Danielle rode their bikes to the Pine Bluffs, the top of a mountain near the Delaware River, and prayed together. "We heard, 'Hair studio,'" says Peach. "No more than that. So we obeyed and opened our hair studio, CUT Artisan Hair Design, in October 2012, after saving $60,000." Today the studio grosses nearly $1 million a year.

"If I can do it, any knucklehead can do it," Peach says. "I don't have a college degree. It took me two tries to get my GED."

"If I can do it, any knucklehead can do it."

The key to Peach's success was his faith and making sure any decision he made was right in his heart. He adamantly believes this isn't just about the money. It's about the people his businesses serve. In fact, the mission statement for the salon is, "To love and to serve through Artisan Hair Design."

Peach continues: "Oftentimes as entrepreneurs, we have so many ideas. It can be a bit of a mess. Even after Danielle and I received our direction from God, we went to mentors. They were hard on us and asked the hard questions. My friends were always encouraging. We need them some days to cancel out the voices of our enemies. But the mentors made sure we were making the right decisions for the right reasons."

Today Peach and Danielle have an advisory board of five people, but there are really ten, because they include the unofficial members of the board—the spouses. "It's harder to fool many than one," Peach emphasizes. "As you grow, you need more counsel." As it says in Proverbs 11:14, "Where there is no counsel, the people fall: but in the multitude of counselors there is safety."

Peach, now thirty-two years old, manages the holding company and has removed himself from the day-to-day activities of the four companies under this umbrella: CUT Artisan Hair Design, Hardy's Coffee Roastery, Hardy's Coffee Bar, and a bakery named Parchment, which he launched in October 2019 to help his brother, who had recently lost his job. "To love and to serve."

"We love helping people," Peach concludes. "I was a drug addict before I met God. I used just about everything but heroin to cover up my pain. Many of our employees are former addicts as well."

Employees who follow Peach's work ethic can become business owners through a variety of unique programs. Apprentices can seek a career path that leads to ownership and a place to work and earn (and even reside in some business models); then they can become full owners.

One such career path is a journey from hair stylist to owner. Peach also taps into the tiny house movement for coffee shops and roasteries with a franchise model, which I will profile in the food and beverage section.

"Entrepreneurs are a lot like drug addicts, because they're willing to take risks," says Peach. "Addicts are misguided in the risks they take, but if they take risks for the right reasons, many will succeed."

Peach and his vision provide the guidance often missing in an addict's life. "My wife and I are living an amazing ride. We worked really, really hard for the first couple of years, and we still do. It just looks different now," Peach says. "It's all by God's watching over and directing our lives and us being obedient."

Earn, Learn, and Then Launch

There are opportunities available to you that represent a career pathing strategy, where you take advantage of internship or apprenticeship offerings that are stepping-stones to your dream business. The following opportunity that Peach has created is one such career path that leads to ownership. In another section, I'll share two similar apprentice-to-owner businesses that Peach has created around the specialty coffee industry.

Business 1: *Hair Studio*

After touring in a rock band and losing himself in the drug culture and ensuing debt, Peach, along with his wife, gave their lives to God and ultimately felt called to open a hair studio, CUT Artisan Hair Design. Taking it further, they committed to hiring people in recovery, especially second chancers coming out of Adult and Teen Challenge Centers, whose goal is "to create locally sustainable programs where men, women, boys, and girls find lasting freedom from addiction and discover the life-changing power of Jesus Christ," according to their website.

"Reentering life after rehab is tough," says Peach. "Nobody wants to hire a recovered addict." Moved by empathy for these individuals, Peach and Danielle created a path for them to find the dignity of self-sufficiency. They used a strategy of love and respect to empower these precious people at the most fragile point of their new, sober life—reengagement with society, family, and career.

Peach and Danielle helped them by offering to sponsor and mentor them through the education process related to cosmetology and hairstyling licensing. Those that chose this path had jobs waiting for them in the studio. Pete and Danielle even took some of these folks into their home after their time in the halfway house, offering them a spare room or basement apartment to live while they were getting on their feet.

CUT Artisan Hair Design is based in New Jersey, so stylists must adhere to requirements for the New Jersey State Board of Cosmetology and Hairstyling. Licensing requires that the individual be at least seventeen years of age, provide proof of successful completion of high school or GED and 1,200 hours of instruction in cosmetology and hairstyling at an approved school, and pass a test administered by the board.

Once they gain knowledge and learn the responsibilities of the business, the stylists are eligible to earn a franchise in a satellite location. Once they've proven their dedication to a life of service, Peach funds the startup so that the new entrepreneur can work off the startup cost and have full ownership after a few years.

Take a moment and consider this: There are people in your community who want to help you get your GED, learn a trade, and get you started in your own business. Many who embrace a life of service are called to assist even the most unfortunate and downtrodden. You always have hope, my friend, and that hope could live right next door. There are always opportunities to improve your life, as long as you're open to receiving it.

Parting Thoughts

Almost everything I have ever written about business is based on self-determination and independence, but there's a slightly different magic at work here: there are people out there who want to come alongside you, put an arm around you, and support your independence. People like Peach and Danielle are in your community; they love God and others and want to empower you to do better, make a new start, and find the dignity of self-reliance. They don't know you, but they love you. They are deeply committed to helping others grow, improve, and realize their dreams. They are angels called by God to undergird your dreams, to put the wind under your wings—to help you fly.

For many entrepreneurs, a more structured career path like this is the most appropriate road to success. Sometimes you "get by with a little help from your friends." Sometimes, even if you're independent and a self-starter, it's OK to accept help, and to partner with those that God has placed to come alongside you in your quest. Check out the two examples below.

Barber in a Bag and Hair Aid are two nonprofit organizations combining hair and a helping hand. According to Hair Aid, they work "globally to make a difference and create change by teaching people living in poverty the skill of hair cutting. Once they've been trained people can start their own microbusiness, cutting hair in their own communities, earning money. With money, they can support their families by buying fresh water and food, educate their children and move into housing. 5500+ people have been trained by Hair Aid since 2010." (Hair Aid's hashtag is #changingtheworldone haircutatatime.)

When I talked to Madison Dufour, the founder of Barber in a Bag, she shared the story of a single mother who signed up for the haircutting school in Southeast Asia. The mom had twin three-year old children who were climbing all over her, one on a leg and another around her neck, while she was trying to complete her final exam—a haircut! With comb and scissors in hand, the mom was determined to complete her training and obtain a certificate. Everyone survived, thank God, and the single mother now has training so she can go out and start a business of her own.

Look around you. These angels are hidden in plain sight. People like Madison are ready to spend their time and treasure to help you succeed.

How to Get Started

Why consider an apprenticelike relationship or apprenticeship job such as Peach offers? According to apprenticeship.gov, "through an apprenticeship program, you can obtain paid, relevant workplace experience while acquiring the skills and credentials that employers value. Fully 94 percent of apprentices who complete an apprenticeship retain employment, with an average annual salary of $70,000."

There are additional benefits to considering this choice:

- **Earn as you learn,** with guaranteed wage increases as you learn more skills.
- **Credentials.** Receive an industry-recognized and portable credential, such as a stylist or cosmetology license, as well as other technical or trade credentials in other industries.
- **Jump-start your career** as you ease the transition from school to career by working and learning at the same time.
- **Education.** Gain workplace-relevant skills in the field of your choice through on-the-job learning.
- **Degree potential.** You can gain academic credit towards a college degree for the skills you learn while avoiding student debt. Some employers will pay for your college.
- **Mentorship.** You will likely connect with mentors in your chosen field who want to help you advance your career.

There are several places you can look for apprenticeship and internship opportunities. They may include preapprenticeship training programs, apprenticeship programs, internships, manager training, franchisee grooming, and managing partner programs (10 percent ownership) such as those available at Bonefish Grill. First, look for people in your community, like Peach and Danielle, who want to help you get started. In addition, there are online sources to look for opportunities, such as:

1. United States Department of Labor Apprenticeship Finder: https://www.apprenticeship.gov/apprenticeship-finder.

2. State-registered programs. Twenty-five states, the District of Columbia, and Puerto Rico offer state registered programs directories. The remaining twenty-five states use the DOL directory above. Go to the Education Commission of the States for a comparison of all 50 states with links to each state program: https://c0arw235.caspio.com/dp/b7f930001aeba2373e734db1bf8e.

3. If you are between the ages of sixteen and twenty-four, the Jobs Corps offers free training for preapprentice candidates. If you want to create a woodworking business but don't have the skills, you can begin with a Job Corps preapprentice training program, then take an apprenticeship as a carpenter, which will prepare you to open your own business down the road.

Career Pathing

Career pathing is a process you can use to map the course for your career development and entrepreneurial launch. It will be important for you to understand what knowledge, skills, character traits, and experience you will need to advance your plan to independence. Take a look in the mirror, assess your goals, as well as the skills and knowledge you have today, and compare them to what you will need to achieve those goals. You'll need a plan for personal and professional development. Write it down, then carry it out.

Each simple job that you do *well* is preparing you for your dream business.

- Becoming a great grass cutter is the first step toward your dream business as an arborist or outdoor designer (see Kathy Agresto's story in business 21).
- Becoming a good mechanic's apprentice is the first step to starting your mobile mechanic business.
- Becoming a great editor's apprentice at DreamWorks TV may be the first step toward your video or movie production company.

Everybody is different. If you want to start a business tomorrow morning—do it! If you think you want to get some education and experience under your belt first, then plotting a career path may be your best first step.

Peach's Tips and Techniques

1. "You've got to humble yourself and equally you've got to have confidence," shares Peach. "I read this verse all the time: 'Trust in the Lord with all your heart and lean not on your own understanding' (Proverbs 3:5), and I had to keep reminding myself: God has an amazing plan for your life."

2. "You have to get around people who are successful and doing what you want to do—and you have to copy them," Peach advises. "Nothing is original. Steve Jobs said, 'Good engineers invent code. Great engineers steal it.' People who eat, sleep, and breathe their business are happy to show their cards. People want to see you succeed."

3. "You have to make sure this is about people. Our mission statement for the hair studio is to 'love and serve through artisan hair design.' If it's about the money, it won't have meaning. If you take Jesus out of the equation, you have a problem. If you do something without God's calling, it will be a failure."

4. Peach believes that if you can show people your vision, they'll grab it. "You have to have a product to sell, and then you have to perfect that product, and you have to make more ways for people to spend money faster."

Horizontal Growth

To achieve horizontal growth as a stylist or cosmetologist, you will gradually experiment with providing a wider range of products to your clients and/or expanding your activities to other geographic areas. Here are some examples:

1. Providing a wider range of products and services may include learning techniques that are new to you, such as hair coloring, weaves and extensions, eyebrow tinting, and threading. It may also include makeup art for special events or theatrical and performance clients.

2. Find a niche and dig into it. Being known for a specialty is often better than being a generalist. The most successful businesses are often ones that provide clients a curated experience rather than the same general services provided by everyone else.

3. You may book a day in a different town or neighborhood to begin building additional clientele outside your home circle. Your core clients will live or work in a ten-minute radius of your primary business location. However, in order to cast a wider net, you will need a satellite location or chair. You can book

three full days in two locations rather than having six sparsely booked days in one location.

FOR SALON OWNERS:

1. Expand the services you offer, as noted above, but be careful to avoid related business departments that turn into time sucks: business niches that seem like a good idea but ultimately never bring an adequate return on investment (ROI). Some salons do well by adding nails, facials, or massages. If you try one approach and it doesn't work out, drop it and move on quickly. You may succeed with nails but not with massage. That's OK; work to your strength, but don't hang on to an unprofitable supplementary service. Not every good idea is a profitable idea.

2. Expand the number of chairs and stylists. This is your quickest path to growth, but again, be careful. If you fail to create an environment or business culture that people like, you won't be able to fill your chairs. Be sure you want to spend time with the people you invite into your space. Through an interview and vetting process, ensure that you share values and work ethic, or else these new additions will also become vampires that will suck the life and time out of you. They will cost you more than you bargained for.

3. Build a niche and grow it. Most successful businesses are known for a specialty, not for being generalists. Your niche may be color, razor fades, a male-oriented, sports-themed environment, or high-end ambiance, with wine and cheese for customers. As you focus on a client type, you get better at delivering a great experience to those clients, which will in turn increase customer retention, growth, and profit margins.

4. Once you perfect your business model, employee retention, marketing, and client acquisition, you may seek to add satellite locations and grow your business exponentially. Be sure you get the business model, system, and processes running like a Swiss watch before you expand. You want a duplicable model to expand upon. Opening a new location will not often save an unprofitable first location (unless that first location becomes impaired). Caution: you also need to have adequate capital, good people on your team, and the bandwidth to handle the expansion. Many profitable businesses end up sinking themselves because they lacked adequate capital or people power to complete an expansion. Instead, they diluted their already good business. Proceed with care, and operate from strength.

Vertical Growth

1. Take advantage of an apprenticeship such as Peach and Danielle offer. You will grow vertically from expanding a client base to owning your own salon, where you are profiting from the chairs of other stylists as well as from the sale of hair and skin care products.

2. If you rent a chair or work in a salon today, you can move to independence quickly in a shared suite arrangement, in such locations as Phenix Salon Suites or Sola Salon Studios, which claim you can *be in business for yourself, but not by yourself.* This is an easy move from employee to entrepreneur, because the suite provider is creating the infrastructure that is difficult for many first-time entrepreneurs to accomplish: the commercial lease, interior buildout, sinks, chairs, towel service, online booking software, etc.

3. If your thing is real estate, you may want to break into the salon suite space by being the landlord to stylists. You can develop the

real estate yourself or sublease a space. A cottage industry has sprung up around this market niche, complete with consultants like Salon Suite Partners or Salon Suites Consulting.

Variations

The following businesses can be launched following the same or similar principles, business plan, and marketing as described above.

Business 2: *Anti-Aging Practice*

This business offers methods and products to fight the effects of aging. Think in terms of cryotherapy, dermaplaning, and more. *Entrepreneur* magazine calls this "the new startup frontier." Over 75 million baby boomers will be entering retirement over the next decade, and they control over 70 percent of the wealth in America. The anti-aging industry is predicted to reach $50 billion by 2021, according to Statista. One example of an anti-aging business opportunity is through MONAT, a company that supports independent marketers and grew its sales from $42 million to $365 million from 2016 to 2019. The company provides training, marketing, and your own e-commerce online store.

Business 3: *Anti-Tan Treatment*

Beauty care and skin care treatment to combat the effects of sun exposure. Mobile spray tanning businesses are a thing! (Internet search: mobile+spray+tan+businesses.) You will find many options, and the equipment manufacturers will train you for free.

Business 4: *Aromatherapy Treatments*

Consider this option as an add-on to other treatments using natural, aromatic essential oils. (See chapter 19 for possible companies to partner with.)

Business 5: *Beauty Blog*

The perfect work-from-home business. You will need writing skills and time. Even if you only have a cursory knowledge of the beauty business, you can interview experts and report on current developments in this business segment. It's a great way to be an influencer. From there, you can increase your visibility, leading to additional clients, speaking offers, and more. After a time, you'll have enough material to turn those blogs into a book, leading to even more visibility and another stream of income.

One of the best places to start if you want to monetize your blog is WordPress.org (*not* WordPress.com). WordPress.org is the most popular way to make a blog or website, according to technology survey site W³Techs. You will have thousands of free themes and tens of thousands of free plug-ins, like the website builder eCommerce, and contact forms. You don't need any technical knowledge to set it up, and you will own your content and data.

WordPress.org does require you to self-host, which means you'll need to add the hosting for $3–$6 per month at the likes of DreamHost, Bluehost, or GoDaddy.

WordPress.com, which is often confused for WordPress.org, is a hosting service. It is owned by Automattic, a company started by the cofounder of WordPress. Here are some of the differences:

WordPress.org	WordPress.com
Free	Monthly Subscription
Own Your Site	Potential Censorship
Ad-Free	Ads on your pages
Customized	Templated
Monetized	No Monetization
Web Store	No Web Store
Google Analytics	WordPress.com Analytics
Premium Content Memberships	No Premium Sites
Plug-ins	No Plug-ins
Own the House	Rent the House

Have fun setting up your look, and then start writing!

Business 6: *Beauty Product Marketing*

Read more about this business idea in the Direct Sales section. I'll give you numerous examples and wholesale partners.

Business 7: *Exhibition Organizer*

Are you a great organizer or event planner? Then it's time to hit the road and put on shows and exhibitions, with beauty professionals and aspiring models as stakeholders and with talent recruiters and advertising professionals as constituents. Kate Dodd has written a terrific blog post called "Planning an Expo: What You Need to Know," which provides a checklist for exhibition planning. The company for which she writes, Event Tech Group, also has a tool for hosting a virtual exhibition, conference, or fashion show.

In a post Covid-19 world, virtual exhibitions and fashion, hair, or beauty shows may be an extremely relevant innovation. Check out eventtechsoftware.com/virtualconference.

Business 8: *Image Consultant*

This is a great way to take your sense of style and use it to advise clients about makeovers, clothing, fitness, and poise. No storefront needed. You can even build a membership site by offering virtual and video consulting. Start on social media at no cost to you. When you've built up a following, you can create your own website.

Business 9: *Makeup Artist*

Nearly everyone wants to look extra special at big life events. Team up with bridal consultants, photographers, and similar professionals to share the word about your talents.

Business 10: *Manicurist and Pedicurist*

This mimics the career path for stylists and cosmetology.

Business 11: *Mobile Facial Spa*

Bring specialty skin care to the busy consumer. There is anecdotal evidence that this is a strong and growing trend. Organization is key. Mobile facial providers share these tips: Bring a small rice cooker or steamer to use as a source for warm and hot water (so you don't need to run back and forth to the client's sink). Use a small foldaway trolley or handcart, massage couch, couch roll, folding stool, towels, small towels or flannels, and your mobile phone with a Bluetooth battery-operated speaker for mood music. You'll also need cleansers, masks, creams, and other products. Stick to a ten-mile radius (you can also choose to charge an additional $5 or so if you go outside your radius), and have a minimum callout charge. Encourage clients to share the callout charge by inviting a friend or having a pamper party.

Business 12: *Specialty Soap Making*

Danielle Vincent of Outlaw Soaps left the corporate life to provide body care products that tantalize the senses.

Danielle spent much of her career as a product manager at corporations such as OWN: The Oprah Winfrey Network, ABC, and others. Yet Danielle wasn't living life to the fullest. Living in downtown Los Angeles, she rarely ventured into the natural settings of Joshua Tree National Park and Lake Hughes, just an hour or so away from the "concrete warehouse" in which she lived.

"I felt like if I just had a little connection to the places I loved, that maybe I could be inspired and motivated to go there more often," says Danielle. "If I had their scent on me, that I would be carrying a little patch of them with me, reminding me why I was alive," she shares on her Facebook page. From Danielle's desire to have a deeper connection with nature, Outlaw Soaps, "For Adventurous People, by Adventurous People," was born in March 2013.

"Outlaw Soaps is a way to connect yourself with happy memories, good places, inspiring environments, and, more than anything, to remind you to live your best life (thanks for that, Oprah)," Danielle writes on her Facebook page. "All of our scents, including desert sage (Lust in the Dust sagebrush-inspired soap), whiskey (Hair of the Dog whiskey-inspired soap) and all the others (Unicorn Poop is its own story) are designed just to get you outside and remind you the daily grind is not the grind of your life."

This rapidly growing company in Reno, Nevada, has a large and loyal customer base and partners with "all Northern California Whole Foods Markets and dozens of boutiques and gift shops across the US," says Danielle on her LinkedIn page. They've been "featured in *Cowboys & Indians Magazine, Yahoo!, WIRED Magazine, Food Network Magazine, VICE Magazine, Oprah.com, Thrillist,* and many other taste-maker publications."

Although Danielle and her partner in life and business, Russ Vincent, started out making soaps, their line of sundries has expanded to include body wash, deodorant, lotions, colognes, and much more. The products sport Wild West–inspired names, such as "The Badlands," "Blazing Saddles," "Calamity Jane," and "Home on the Range." In addition to individual products, there are also gift sets, subscription boxes, and other choices. (See chapter 17 for more on creating subscription boxes.)

To find out more about the products of this adventurous team, visit Outlaw Soaps at https://liveoutlaw.com/collections/the-everything.

Mini–Business Plan

At the end of this book, I have provided a mini–business plan for you to fill out. Here are some pointers for working with it, using haircutters and cosmetologists as examples.

Story. In the beginning, your value proposition—your story—is your humility and hard work. You will gain the knowledge and experience to launch, own, and operate a high-end salon with little or no money invested.

Inventory. Your assets are the willingness to work, dedication, sacrifice, and the commitment to stay the course for multiple years while you gain the knowledge and experience to be a first-class entrepreneur.

Ideal client. Mass-affluent consumers in a white-collar community where you want to live and work. (See Glossary for "mass-affluent.")

Funding. Via the franchisor in the beginning.

Supply chain. Via the franchisor. They usually supply all the equipment and beauty products.

Marketing. Guided by the franchisor. In addition, promote yourself online and through social media, such as Instagram, Facebook, and LinkedIn. If you can post nice-looking YouTube videos showing your specialty cut, color, or extension, you can really build an audience. (Check out makeup artist Michelle Phan on YouTube. With 8.9 million followers and over a billion lifetime views, Michelle has built a beauty empire beginning with a single viral video, "How to Get Lady Gaga Eyes.") Remember, initially, your brand is *you*.

Drive your Google rating. First, be sure you have a listing, even as a stylist (you don't have to be a company; just promote *you*), and encourage your loyal clients to rate you and write reviews. People looking for a new stylist will often Google the service. They will almost always sort or rank their choices by stars and reviews.

Instagram is solid gold for stylists. Take pictures of your best work and happy customers and then post them. Be sure to obtain clients' permission first.

Yelp is also a great place to list your services.

Sell gift cards or certificates.

Start a referral program. Provide your current clients with a handful of business cards for their friends, families, and coworkers.

Create a **"frequent flyer" program**.

Use **booking software**, which automatically sends appointment reminders to clients via email or text.

Turn certain services into **subscriptions**. For example, a monthly subscription provides the client with eyebrows for life!

Start **blogging** by sharing your expertise on products, cuts for certain types of hair, and similar topics.

For one example, read "Leaving the Cubicle to Start a $23K/Month Soap Company" on the StarterStory website.

3

The Work of Your Hand

And whatever you do, do it heartily,
as to the Lord and not to men.
—COLOSSIANS 3:23

In every community, people need help in maintaining, organizing, and improving their homes, gardens, businesses, and lives. Yet not everyone has time to tend to the home or the yard when they're working full-time, raising their children, or traveling for business or pleasure. Some choose to put more time into their volunteer endeavors. And not everyone has the talent or the patience to create works of art out of simple placement of furniture or plants, or even organizing their possessions and deciding what to keep, what to donate, and what to send off to the dump.

Here you'll meet one woman who, through word of mouth, began her business simply by tending to her neighbors' condos while they were out of town. Simple tasks such as getting the mail, watering the plants, and arranging for maintenance of appliances sparked an even bigger business for Donna Fabbri, who now oversees estates sales, downsizing, and similar services, not only for her neighbors but in communities beyond.

Business 13: *Perfecto! by Donna Fabbri*

At fifty years old, Donna Fabbri experienced several life-changing events. Her second marriage ended in divorce, her mom died, and life wasn't making much sense anymore. To get clarity on all the change, she left San Francisco, where she had been working as an executive assistant to the CEO of Monster Cable, and moved to San Diego to regroup.

"I had no intentions of staying here. I just needed to get away," says Donna. The mother of two adult children, she had never lived on her own. Raised in a traditional Italian family, all she ever knew to do was to get married and care for the people around her. "I had to learn about me, about who I am," she explains.

Prior to her move, Donna had been taking care of her father. "I don't regret the time spent with my father," she reflects. "I would do it again. But I had to figure out what I wanted to do with my life. It took a good year and a half before I could see the light." That light came to her in the form of synchronistic events.

For about three months, Donna was living at the Marriott Marquis, paying her way with a divorce settlement. Soon she learned that condos were being rented at City Front Terrace for about $1,200 a month—less than she was paying for her hotel stay. So she moved to the elegant brick high-rise, in downtown San Diego's Marina District. A short time later, the condo units were put on the market, and the sales manager elicited Donna's assistance in obtaining quotes for home theater systems, which many buyers had requested.

This task fit perfectly within Donna's experience, since the Fortune 500 company that she had worked for did exactly that. Before long, she was the project manager for the installations, and then one thing led to another. Residents, many of whom were part-timers, needed assistance with things like walking the dog, buying groceries, and checking the mail. Donna stepped up and did what she does so well—take care of people.

"Being a personal assistant and concierge helped me get the larger jobs," explains Donna, owner of Perfecto!, a company that provides full-service condo, house, and estate management, including remodels of all sizes, deliveries and installations, moving in, moving out, estate sales, and turnkey moves, providing complete unpacking, with beds made and groceries in the refrigerator. Her company has such a good reputation that Donna often finds herself going to other cities, such as Seattle and San Francisco, to oversee projects. Of late, she has been assisting people in downsizing because of deaths, foreclosures, divorces, and bankruptcies.

Donna's business was built on word of mouth because of her impeccable work ethic and customer service. Her clients trust her, and she receives numerous referrals from estate lawyers and real estate professionals. Many times, she's called upon to assist those nearing the end of their lives to get their affairs in order. She helps them go through all of their paperwork and belongings to reduce their families' burden.

"I love this work," says Donna. "It's what my instinct is and what I was born and raised to do. It comes natural to me, and I'm not judgmental."

While Donna is the main go-between for the client and the service providers, she no longer does the heavy lifting. She has enlisted a small crew of individuals, mainly military moms, who have caring personalities and can handle the stress from clients, who often have their own life challenges.

Dona doesn't always think of the pressures of her work as bad. Many of her client experiences are rewarding. Recently some clients were in Europe for a big life event. During their vacation, their condo sold, and they had to vacate the premises within fifteen days. Donna stepped in with her crew, packing everything and carting it off to storage so that the couple could carry on with their celebration.

"I made a difference in their lives, and they trusted me," Donna shares. That story has been repeated many times. One Christmas she was asked to prepare a family condo for the holiday, including shopping for and wrapping gifts and putting up the tree.

With twenty years in her ever-evolving business, Donna has many stories to tell, including her own challenges. Creating a steady income topped the list. Initially, many of her clients only needed her services when they were out of town and she didn't have them on retainer. "This is still an issue," she says. "And I have to be very aware of the balance between my short-term clients and the projects that take three to six months." Finding good people to work with was also difficult. "I wanted people who cared about what I do and care about my clients, like I do. My whole company could be ruined by the wrong people."

Luckily, Donna has found trusted employees the same way she has grown her business: through word of mouth referrals. They demonstrated their loyalty to Donna and her clients during a recent health crisis, when Donna was faced with either shutting the business down all together or taking a sabbatical. Instead, her team offered to step in and keep her business running. With her health returned, she's now back at the helm and eager to see where the tides of life will take Perfecto! next.

For more about Donna Fabbri and Perfecto!, visit her website: perfectosd.com.

How to Get Started

Let's begin with the sequence of events that led to Donna's startup: she began helping with a single job. That first home theater installation was the catalyst for referrals, which led to more outsourced jobs because of her dependability and caring personality. She continued to receive more referrals and jobs, and her successful completion of those jobs led to referrals for new jobs beyond the scope of the original audio installation (horizontal growth).

You will see the same pattern repeated throughout this book: people demonstrate faithfulness and good stewardship in seemingly mundane and unglamorous tasks. This leads to the next thing, which leads to a better thing, which ultimately leads to exponential growth and success. The parable of the talents is being lived out before our eyes: do your absolute best with what you've been entrusted, and you will receive ten times more. Be a good steward with your $100, and you will soon be stewarding $1 million.

The great majority of people in this world are *not* successful because they are *not* faithful with what God has given them, and they never receive the next level of responsibility. They don't move to their next stepping-stone. They don't reach for the next rung on the ladder of life. Be faithful in the little things, and God will be faithful in entrusting you with the big things. It's not just Providence: the natural laws of reciprocity and the markets favor the good steward.

This business, like many others, began with performing simple outsourced jobs for a single person, like Donna helping condo owners with little projects. Another example is Peach painting a deck; still another is Kathi Burns' Organized and Energized business, dedicated to organizing closets. The key to success is they did that simple job well, and it led to the next job. Once you have momentum, you can build your small business into a bigger business. If you don't succeed at the first few efforts, don't get discouraged or give up. The law of large numbers is in your favor. Just keep trying, and you'll eventually succeed.

As you read the following extremely diverse group of business ideas in this chapter, remember to find your niche and perform your job well. You will easily get the next job (or contract), and the next one, and the next one, and then the big ones! Each of these businesses, ranging from household projects to outdoor maintenance, can lead to a big, profitable enterprise if done well. But if you're a screw-up and make excuses, you're not going to get the next job, and you won't be able to grow a business from thin air. Your diligence is key to your success, so even if you lose money on the first couple of jobs, do your best, and win the next contract. Remember, always underpromise and overdeliver. Exceed expectations in everything you do. Not only will you have a profitable business, but you will find success in finance, marriage, childrearing, relationships, and altruism. Be *that* guy. Be *that* gal.

Starting a business like these is easy: Find a job that needs being done. Do it well and move on to the next one.

Tips and Techniques for Building Your Business

1. Work for someone in the same industry first. You'll learn firsthand what you'll need to know when you launch your own business.
2. Make sure you're choosing a business sector that you like and that fits your lifestyle.
3. Network. Connect with anyone and everyone you know.

4. Put your house in order: website, business cards, licensing, insurance, and similar details. Try not to look like a startup or a rank amateur. Fake it till you make it!

Horizontal Growth

Add more employees or contractors in more buildings and locations.

Vertical Growth

Create a service, website, or app that places concierges in other buildings. You become the hub for clients and concierges, collecting a fee for each paid service.

Variations
Indoors

Business 14: *Housecleaning Service*

With very little up-front investment for cleaning supplies and equipment, you can begin earning between $25 and $50 per hour, depending on your location. You can charge even more for seasonal deep cleaning or move-out or event cleanup. Whether you're serving the average houseowner (residential) or a business owner (commercial), be sure to be punctual, consistent, and dependable. Build trust and relationships, and your profits will soar.

If you go to Care.com, you can look up a variety of services in your community: home care, child care, tutoring, senior care, pet care, and housekeeping. If you look at the housekeeping section, you will see rates ranging from $13 to $50 per hour.

This idea has got to have the lowest barrier to entry of any business in this book. Anybody can clean. You don't need to know how to read, type, or write computer code—just clean. The question is, are you willing? Are you willing to clean someone else's house or office in order to start your business? If you are willing and able, you can start working by the hour, but I'd rather see you estimate how long it will take per job and bid each location by the job. This way, you're establishing a business relationship rather than becoming an employee at will, or worse yet, a servant. If you're weirded out by cleaning someone's house, try bidding office, commercial, ware-house, or other jobs. My cousin did well cleaning ducts, especially restaurant vents and ducts, which were nasty but paid big bucks. His team would do the work overnight, from midnight to 6:00 a.m.

You may be saying to yourself, "I'm not going to be someone's maid," but you're not looking at the big picture. You've got to start small and with humility, but the upside is huge. There are very few straight-up domestic employees anymore, so most cleaning and maintenance jobs are handled by contract companies. It's good business.

Let's look at a company that cleans one of my properties. They charge approximately $183 per visit. They usually send a crew of 2–3 people, who are in and out in 2 hours. They pay them $13 per hour (I asked). So here is the profit and loss scenario: Each crew of 3 completes 3–4 jobs per day, costing the owner of the business approximately $54 per hour per crew, or $374 per day. (I used the $13 per hour and added 20 percent for payroll taxes and costs, assuming no benefits). Each job, if it is the same as my location, brings reve-nue of $188. Four of those in a day is $752. Less the $374 labor cost, that leaves a profit of $378 per day. Multiply that by approximately 4 crews and 250 working days in the year, and you have a gross profit of $378,000 per year. You can subtract 10–20 percent for supplies and overhead, and you're left with $340,000–$302,400 per year.

Business 15: *Window Cleaning Service*

According to Craig Wallen, author of *Start Your Own Window Cleaning Business,* "The average window cleaner makes $50 to $70 per hour, so just by working four Saturdays a month, you could be bringing in an extra $1,400 to $2,000 next month!" (https://www.profitablewindowcleaning.com/). His advice is, pick your niche, partner with lumberyards and glass companies, and begin earning even before you quit your day job.

My son took a summer job with his buddy working for a company called the Transparent Cleaning Co., whose slogan is "Honest & Good." The owner allows the boys to bid their own jobs, using a formula of a given amount per windowpane, and then pays them 30 percent of the job's price. The boys prepare their bids on their iPhone, in the cloud, on a template the owner created in Google sheets. What a great combination of old-school techniques and cloud computing!

My son is seventeen years old and made nearly $500 one week. If you launched this business yourself, you've earned more than $1,500 for the week, which is an annual rate of $75,000 per year (assuming a fifty-week working year). If you were running 3 crews like this company, your retention would be $152,000 on an annualized basis. That's just on windows. They do gutters and interior cleaning as well.

Business 16: *Interior Decorator*

If you have an eye for furniture placement, color, texture, and similar details, you'll fit right into this growing industry. Many people want to upgrade the look of their homes but have neither the time nor talent to do so. They may have jotted down numerous ideas from their favorite do-it-yourself decorating shows but don't know where to start. This is where you come in. Stage a friend's house for free, take a few photos, grab a testimonial, and let people know you're in business. Here you can make between $35 and $50 per hour.

Traditional interior decorating is a crowded space, but if you're good with color, style, decor selection, and staging, you can build a reputation in your community, not only among homeowners but among important business partners and centers of influence such as contractors and landlords. If you're going to leverage your interior decorating up from a hobby to a viable business, cultivating these relationships in the business community is important. You can wait for housewives to call you for decorating tips, or you can turbo-charge the business by becoming the go-to person for architects and contractors who are consulting with custom-build clients, and landlords who may recommend you to residential and commercial tenants.

There is a loose connection between this traditional interior decorating activity and the following opportunities available in relation to holidays, parties, and events (see business plans 17, holiday decorator; 18, event facilitator; and 20, landscape maintenance and design). Your sense of style, aesthetic, placement, space, and utilization of elements can morph into one or a combination of these businesses.

Business 17: *Holiday Decorator*

One of my cousins started installing Christmas lights as a side hustle during his Christmas break from his day job. He and his partners were stunned by the amount of money they were making. There was so much demand for installations that they couldn't keep up.

As I dug deeper into this business model, I found three types of entrepreneurs: part-timers, who just do installations during the holiday season; landscapers and housecleaning crews, who work seasonally; and full-timers who have expanded their side gig into a year-round enterprise, not only installing holiday decorations but becoming an outsourcer for all kinds of decorations, ranging from different holiday decors (Christmas, Hanukkah, Thanksgiving, Halloween, and Easter) to party and event decor, which is very lucrative (see the following business plans: 18, special event facilitator; and 19, supplier). If you can break into corporate event theming and facilitating, it can be big business.

Business 18: *Event and Party Facilitator*

Simple theme-oriented decorating can grow into decorating for special events. Someone may want to throw a party, conference, or exhibition at a rented event center or hotel ballroom but may not have the time or inclination to decorate it to their theme.

Here is your opportunity! You can decorate the location for the event. A couple of cases of leis, fake palm trees, and grass skirts, and you are on your way to theming a luau for your client's event. Begin with manageable-sized parties and graduate to business events.

Event facilitators work in four areas: celebrations (weddings, graduations, anniversaries), education (conferences and meetings), promotions (product launches and fashion shows), and commemorations (memorials, political rallies, and other such events).

In this field, you may be coordinating every aspect of an event from inviting guests, planning the menu, and hiring the caterer to arranging for transportation and lodging. You can team up with a rental business for tables, chairs, arbors, and other party needs, and with caterers, photographers, hotels, and Airbnb hosts to expand your services and marketing efforts. If weddings are your niche, you could even become an officiant and join couples in matrimony.

Your earnings are based not only on your hourly rate but on a "cost-plus" method, whereby you charge 15–20 percent above the cost for all the services involved in putting together a spectacular event.

Enliven Production Group is a company that has evolved into a multivenue producer of events. They produce killer on-site events as well as polished, professional virtual events, which is very important in a post-Covid business world. This is a later stage of the business growth cycle, showing how you can grow from small decor jobs to staging to full production. You can begin with decorating homes and businesses, grow into parties, and from there graduate to special events, conferences, and exhibitions. As a facilitator of events, you may be renting most of your equipment and props, while providing the creativity and labor to set up and tear down the decorations and equipment. We'll talk about stockpiling and renting this equipment in the next chapter.

Another area of subspecialty in the event planning arena is audio, video, and lighting. If you are throwing a party, conference, or special event, you may want it well illuminated and recorded. If so, you'll look to a company like OMNIvision event services in Carlisle, U.K. (omnivision.om.org), which produces live events, handles postproduction (creating edited audio and video recordings after your event), and provides international field coverage for nonprofits worldwide, with strength in Europe (their production trucks can travel through the Chunnel and reach almost any place in Western Europe to produce high-quality events). Their big trucks and vans carry not only microphones, lights, and cameras but a self-contained director's booth and editing studio. Another interesting twist on OMNIvision's business model is that it is a nonprofit whose purpose is to support the Christian nonprofits who are its clients. Their videographers, editors, and production managers are all volunteers! If you have a talent for audio, video, and lighting, you may have a future in electronic event services.

When it comes to party planning, think fun! Work with compatible vendors to provide enjoyable activities and food at the party. In addition to the usual dunking or photo booths, which you can rent, you may want to include a fun dessert vendor like Josh & John's Scoop Bus (www.scoopbus.com), a 1968 VW microbus, painted in vivid colors, whose side opens up like a clamshell to serve ice cream to guests. Other ideas are a rustic S'mores bar, taco cart, or a Kona Ice shaved ice truck (Kona offers franchises too: ownakona.com).

Vertical Growth

You may find that you want to grow the business vertically from facilitating events into supplying special event equipment and props, as we'll see in the next profile.

Business 19: *Event and Party Supplier*

Cover It Up in London is an event rigging company that started in 2000 with just three people. Today their staff of twenty-five provides rentals, setups, and takedowns of stage and theater curtains, venue drapery, and event drapes throughout the U.K. and Europe. The simplest forms of event drapery are pipe and drape sets: a simple set of connecting pipes, with a stabilizing plate for feet, upon which you can hang drapes (usually black) as a backdrop for displays, event booths, and staging for speakers or presenters. You commonly see these at conferences, exhibitions, or sports and music events.

As events grow in size and the complexity of their presentations, the need for specialty drapes and customization increases. Experienced companies provide specialty draping such as wedding cabanas, ceiling treatments, dramatic door and window swags, outdoor tent draping, and specialty materials, like satin or beaded curtains.

Quest Events (questevents.com) is an example of a mature company that provides event management and production as well as supplying drapes, props, and equipment.

When you're starting this business in your community, you may begin by planning and producing parties and events. You'll find yourself renting tons of chairs, tables, and tablecloths. I would start the supply side of the business by beginning to accumulate the most common items that people need for events rather than renting them. Six- and eight-foot rectangular tables as well as five-foot round, molded plastic–topped banquet tables are ubiquitous at almost any event. You can buy a bundle of ten of these round tables with a universal table cart for about $1,300 at EventStable.com. You can also buy them one at a time at your local big-box wholesale club. I checked a few rental companies and found the average price to rent the six-foot rectangular table was $10, and $11 for both the eight-food rectangular and five-foot round tables. The cost of tables is between $50 and $100. If we split the difference and use an average price of $75 per table, then you will recapture your investment after eight rentals. If your table survives five years, you will gross $525 on your table if you rent it once per month for the next five years.

Linens rent from $5 to $12 each. The cost of chairs ranges from $12 to $100, and they rent from $5 to $30 each. If you're concentrating on the corporate market, consider purchasing a projector and sound system. Projectors rent for about $125, screens for about $30. You could make back your investment with one rental.

Variations
Outdoors

Business 20: *Landscape Maintenance*

A few years ago, I met a man who became a hunting and fishing buddy. Our kids were the same age, so we enjoyed many a good adventure afield, especially with the kids. He was very private, so he didn't share much about his past, but over time I put this story together.

He was a typically rowdy young man and enjoyed parties and friends, but had no apparent future. His circumstances changed when his father died and left him an old backhoe on a rusty trailer hooked to a pickup truck, with a snowplow on the front. He started doing small landscaping jobs and stayed busy. Because he was a bold and aggressive character, he was not afraid to tackle big tree removal jobs and started to develop a reputation as an arborist.

The work was slow and expensive, however, and required renting a bucket truck to top the trees—removing much of the upper bulk before felling the main trunk. At a certain point he met a Latin landscape laborer, who told him, "You don't need that bucket truck. Me and my friends love to climb trees." He hired the climbers. The business grew quickly, as he was able to remove large trees deftly and reliably, and he began to receive big contracts, such as municipalities and golf courses. In the winter, his company would plow snow for businesses in the area. Eventually he gave the equipment to the climbers, who had worked so hard for him all those years, and they continue the business to this day.

The last time I saw the arborist, he and his wife were raising their kids in a big, beautiful house on a lake, in a good neighborhood, traveling and enjoying life. His diligence in small work gave him success with a bigger business.

Here are a few tips about equipment: Work trucks, backhoes, dump trucks, and other heavy equipment are very easy to acquire if you're not motivated by style or ego. Over the last year, as I was doing research for this book, I would go on Craigslist or auction sites in various towns and cities as well as listings in India, Africa, and Latin America. Used dump trucks and backhoe/front loaders are available for a few thousand dollars (many in the $6,000–$13,000 range).

These are *ugly* trucks! But so what? This book is about hard work, ingenuity, and creativity. Get an old truck, a bucket of paint, and a brush. Make that truck your own! When you're done, put your name on the side, and you're ready to go. You'll soon have enough money to buy a better truck. Many of us have to start humbly and with simplicity. Be faithful with your ugly old truck, and you'll one day have a fleet of new trucks.

Here's a way to get started if you can't afford even a used machine. Many older trucks and loaders are idled. They're sitting on someone's lot, lacking a job, driver, or buyer. Approach the owners, and ask if they'd share the vehicles with you on a day rate basis. When you get a job, pay the owner a percentage. Eventually either you'll create a good working relationship or you'll be able to afford your own equipment.

One of my clients, a dump truck driver, was laid off from a construction company in California. He moved to Texas, bought a dump truck, and for nearly twenty years made a good living as a freelance dirt mover. I don't know what he paid for the truck, but if you can get years, even decades of service from it—well, as my Dad used to say, "That truck doesn't owe you a dime."

Fair warning: the dirt business can be cyclical and often rises and falls with the business cycle. Construction booms during good times and shuts down in bad times. Be prepared for the ebb and flow of the cycle. Don't be afraid to work hard in a dirty business and use it as a building block upon which you build your dream business.

In many jurisdictions, you'll need a commercial driver's license (CDL) to operate a dump or backhoe. Each state has its own requirements. Don't be afraid—obtain your CDL. It may serve you well over time.

My friend's story very much resembles the next one, about a landscape designer and installer. Both started with small, seemingly unglamorous manual labor jobs, excelled in these jobs, and grew their businesses to large, established, profitable enterprises. You can do the same.

Business 21:
Landscape Design and Installation

Kathryn Agresto, a former business management consultant, turned the tables on her career path when she followed a heartfelt longing to dig her hands into the earth and nurture her love of growing herbs and vegetables. In the process, she discovered a whole new clientele to nurture as well.

In 2007, Kathryn founded Native Soil Gardens to support the Orange County, California, farm-to-table movement by guiding restauranteurs to raise their own food. Her first client was chef David Slay's Park Ave Restaurant in Stanton, who uses the on-premises garden to supply his kitchen with fresh vegetables and herbs.

Beginning with just 2,000 square feet of gardening space, Slay expanded the gardens to over 7,000 square feet. Guests of his restaurants—Il Garage and Park Ave—not only enjoy a fine dining experience but get a healthy dose of nature as well. "People take a glass of wine or cocktail out there and enjoy a leisurely stroll before dinner," says Slay.

Kathryn's father instilled the love of fine food and gardening in her soul. In addition to designing gardens for restaurants, she also creates gardens for local corporations and foodies who want their own designer gardens.

"Our mission is to bring the farm garden to an urban setting," she says. To fulfill her mission, Kathryn offers consultations, custom design, and installations. She'll provide instruction on maintenance and harvesting as well. To bring a little nature indoors, she'll add air-cleaning plants, custom-built wall moss art, and transformative interior green designs.

Others who have solicited Kathryn's services include restauranteur and cookbook author Zov Karamardian, *Orange County Register* food writer and cookbook author Cathy Thomas, and Blue Water Grill owner Jim "U."

To find out more about Kathryn and her work, follow her on Facebook (https://www.facebook.com/NativeSoilGardens/) or Instagram (https://www.instagram.com/nativesoilgardens/), or visit her website (http://www.nativesoilgardens.com/).

How to Get Started

Often a great idea must be tested before it catches fire. Find a client that you can work for either for free or at a reduced rate, and then get testimonials from them.

Tips and Techniques for Building Your Business

Do a great job and the word will spread of your business, just as it has for Kathryn and many others in this book.

Horizontal Growth

Kathy has expanded her services to include not only the installation of gardens but also maintenance. In addition, her company does other greenery installation and maintenance at office buildings and the like. She's also expanded into interior greenery (http://www .nativesoilgardens.com/indoor-greenery.html).

Vertical Growth: Nursery

You could begin growing your own plants to sell to the customers for whom you are installing gardens or indoor plants. I met a colorful character in Texas who had a massive nursery, although he had been living the hippie surfer life on a little sandbar on the Gulf Coast just a few years before. One day he was enjoying the smoke of a particular herb, watching the giant seed pods of the Washingtonia palm trees (aka Mexican fan palms) drop their seeds in piles in the summer breeze. There were thousands of seeds, and as he was in an especially happy mood that day, he decided to sweep them all up into bags and start a nursery. A lovely young woman (now his wife) had some land on which he planted his seeds.

Washingtonia palms grow quickly, so he had sellable trees in just a few years. When I met him, his trees were mature, and he had added additional varieties, such as Chinese fan palms and *Cocos plumosa* or Queen palms. He had crews of workers, a tree spade, trucks, and trailers heavy enough to deliver the trees.

During economic expansions, which included lots of new residential and commercial construction, he could not keep up with the demand for trees and was transporting them as far as 350 miles away. Mature palm trees can sell for as much as $1,800 in Florida (all from a seed you can pick up on the street).

Take the time to read and learn about different trees and plants: the time they take to grow and their water, soil, and sunlight requirements. A *Pigifetta elata* or Black Wanga palm from Indonesia can grow from seed to 20 feet in about 4 years, while a Sabal palmetto may take 30 or more years to reach 20 feet in height. *P. elata* starts easily, but only with fresh seeds; soak the seed overnight in warm water, and then sow in containers. Sometimes it germinates in less than a month.

You'll read below about a grain cooperative I started with some wonderful brothers and sisters in Uganda. Their community would also benefit from a nursery. Very few farmers or businesses are patient or well organized enough to maintain nurseries in these sometimes remote agricultural communities. In many emerging economies, I think it's possible to dominate a local or regional market with a well-run nursery.

Variation
Tilapia Farm

I coached an entrepreneur on the remote island of Mindanao in the Philippines on adding tilapia to his modest grove and garden. With very few sources of protein available to them, many of the people in the villages suffer from poor nutrition. As countries develop, especially in Asia and Africa, they add more protein to their diet. Tilapia can be an affordable and accessible source of protein, as well as a booming business for the entrepreneur who meets that need. Refrigeration is minimal in these communities, so fresh daily delivery for your product is the key to success.

I joke with people often that tilapia is one of the easiest of all businesses, because you can raise them in a garbage can. Indeed many urban entrepreneurs and hobbyists raise them in children's swimming pools and trash cans. Of course, all businesses require care and effort, but the tilapia's hardiness makes it easier than most. A pond is the simplest place to raise the fish, and the farm on Mindanao simply diverted a little water from the stream on the property to a plastic-lined impoundment the owner created by building a small dirt dike. You should start small and grow into a larger system.

Purchase fingerlings sized about ¾ inch to 2 inches (don't get smaller) from your local dealer, then introduce them to your new system. The water temperature should be as close to 85°F as possible (80–100°F). Eating slows at 75°F, at 60°F the fish weaken, and they die at 50°F. The perfect recipe for the water is 5–7 ppm (parts per million) oxygen, 7–7.5 ph, no free ammonia, 200–300 ppm nitrate, less than 20 mg/l CO_2, and no chlorine (don't put them in your swimming pool!). Tilapia should be harvestable in about

8 months. Save some of your mature fish as breeders, and you will have a self-sustaining business (https://www.aquanet.com/small -scale-tilapia-farming).

Check out these books from the library to learn more: *A Manual for Tilapia Business Management* by Ram C. Bhujel, or *How to Grow Tilapia For Fun and Profit: A Layperson's Guide to Growing Tilapia to Adulthood Without All the Technical Jargon that Makes Your Head Hurt* by Nigel de Freitas and Jason Arthur.

Variation
Grain Cooperative

While in Uganda, I observed the wonderful work that World Challenge's Poverty Solutions team was doing in the villages surrounding Lira, not far from the South Sudan border. Their Community Health Evangelism (CHE) development program focused on empowering local leaders to train their own people in critical areas such as sanitation, literacy, health, and agriculture. They personified the saying, "Give a man a fish, and he eats for a day. Teach a man to fish, and he will eat for a lifetime."

The community's transformation was visible from the road. Villages where there was no outreach showed the visible signs of prolonged poverty: rundown buildings, trash everywhere, and sparse, ugly fields. The villages where leaders had taken ownership of the program shined with brightly painted homes, clean yards, and green fields surrounded by groves of banana, mango, and pine.

As I studied their agriculture practices, I noted that most of the farms were producing food for family consumption and bartering in their tiny villages. Out of 300,000 CHE participants, I only noted one farm that consistently delivered grain, fruits, and vegetables to market for commercial profit. The ministry leaders themselves attempted to raise rice commercially, but even with the American ministry purchasing the seeds for them, they still failed to turn a profit.

Moving to financial independence is key to community development and maturity. A family grows its way out of poverty, then finds success providing adequate food and shelter security for themselves. The next steps are business success, savings, and the accumulation of multigenerational wealth (through a family farm or business).

My desire to bring training on these key components—*starting a business, saving,* and *accumulation of equity*—to this group of people in northern Uganda was the original spark that kindled my desire to write this book. These people, pulling plows with ropes over their own back, striving to honor God by improving their lives, and bringing the dignity of financial independence to their families, inspired me do my best to provide them a guidebook, a library of ideas with which they and their children can grab on to hope, find their dream, and succeed against all odds.

The Ugandan director of the program, teaching me about the local market, pointed out an imbalance in local grain production. Certain grains were seasonal. Rice, for example, was harvested several months before school started for the year. The locals would consume all the rice in the first couple of months, leaving a scarcity at the beginning of the school year, even though the public schools were the largest buyers of rice in the area. Prices were therefore much higher at beginning of school, but there was little rice available. The roads are terrible, trucks worse, and there is no well-developed rail system. Therefore it's not easy to transport food from other regions into northern Uganda; most bulk food production and consumption are locally based. The director pointed out that very few businesses stored rice and grain for the off months or high-demand seasons and suggested we could store grain to sell during peak consumption periods. So we did!

We put together a cooperative of growers, community leaders, and a couple of Westerners. This structure encouraged local ownership and skin in the game. Westerners can provide a little capital but, more importantly, can teach best practices. Cooperatives are a great model for taking local development efforts, like sustenance farming, to the next level. Entrepreneurial success is critical to community revival and development.

The *Legal Sourcebook for California Cooperatives: Start-up and Administration*, from the Center for Cooperatives at UC Davis (https://cccd.coop/sites/default/files/resources/LegalSourcebook ForCaliforniaCooperatives_0.pdf), is a good source for step-by-step instructions.

Resources for your area can be found online. Here are a few, listed nationally:

The United States. Download the booklet, *Building a Sustainable Business: A Guide to Developing a Business Plan for Farms and Rural Businesses* (https://www.sare.org/resources/building-a-sustainable -business/).

Uganda. See "Revival of Agricultural Cooperatives in Uganda" (https://www.researchgate.net/publication/325896285_Revival_ of_Agricultural_Cooperatives_in_Uganda).

Mexico. See the study "Farmer Cooperatives in Mexico: Case Studies in Jalisco," by Rex Mauricio Romero Paz (https://mro.massey .ac.nz/bitstream/handle/10179/11121/02_whole.pdf?sequence=2& isAllowed=y).

India. See press release, "Cooperatives have the potential to revive agriculture and make it sustainable: vice president" (https://pib.gov.in/Pressreleaseshare.aspx?PRID=1536474).

Variation
Small Space–High Value Plants

Small space–high value plants, such as saffron, lavender, hydrangea, African violets, and Juliet and heritage roses, can provide a good income from even a backyard garden or small greenhouse.

Saffron is the most expensive culinary herb in the world, selling for $5,000 to $10,000 per pound and requiring approximately 50,000 flowers to produce a pound of dried saffron. This herb can be lucrative, because it only takes a quarter acre of land to grow 50,000 flowers. *Gaia's Garden: A Guide to Home-Scale Permaculture*, by Toby Hemenway, and *Urban Homestead: Your Guide to Self-Sufficient Living in the Heart of the City*, by Kelly Coyne and Erik Knutsen, are good resources for specific growing techniques.

Wild-simulated ginseng is another small space–high value crop. You can plant ginseng as an understory on your tree plantation as an alternative to true wild ginseng: it fetches $300– $700 per pound.

4

New Life for Old Stuff

Love your family, work super hard, live your passion.
—GARY VAYNERCHUK, AUTHOR OF
CRUSH IT! WHY NOW IS THE TIME TO CASH IN ON YOUR PASSION

The adage that one man's junk is another man's treasure is as true today as it was when it was first uttered in the 1860s. Whether you put your creativity to work and create something out of discarded items—like skis, cars, and storage containers—or you help an individual or a family clean up their space and sell unwanted items, there's money to be made in reducing, reusing, and recycling.

Business 22: *Colorado Ski Furniture*

Adam Vernon, founder and managing director of this Manitou Springs, Colorado, company, grew up as a downhill ski racer. Later, his love of skiing led him from the corporate world to the world of small business owner.

"Over the years, I had collected a lot of old skis, and I kept seeing people who were making some really ugly Adirondack chairs with skis," says Adam. Inspired by other people's innovations, the Michigan native made his first Adirondack chair.

Initially, repurposing chairs from old skis was a hobby, but friends and family changed that by asking: "Will you make me one?" Soon after, Adam began making chairs to sell on consignment, some of which were on display locally. His small individual enterprise slowly became a business with the help of two buddies—and 10,000 Facebook followers.

Adam was still at work in his corporate job as business took off, but Providence changed all that when he was laid off. "I didn't want to go back," he said. At that time, he had four full-time and two part-time employees.

Business continued to boom, and change became inevitable. "I realized having people in my garage all the time was really annoying," Adam explains. So in 2015, he rented the space at 419 Manitou Avenue in Manitou Springs, at the base of Pike's Peak. In 2018, he bought the property.

Fourteen years after the beginning, the Adirondack chair is the mainstay of the company's product line, which now includes rocking chairs, benches, barstools, doghouses, and tables. Colorado Ski Furniture is now a family affair, with Adam's wife, mom, and kids pitching in. He also has nine painters, who create some of the "coolest" ideas ever, he proudly shares.

The company produces two different Adirondack chairs—tall and medium—which sell for $299 at the low end, with most in the $350–$650 range. Some, which require paint jobs of 25–30 hours, fetch as much as $2,000 each.

Adam discovered horizontal growth opportunities in other raw materials. "We started by using skis for Adirondack chair frames and have branched out into many more repurposed goods, such as barnwood, snowboards, golf clubs, wakeboards, old ski chair-lifts, hockey sticks, water skis, and locally sourced wood," he says. "We handcraft custom furniture to bring the magical memories of mountain living home." He likes to provide variety in order to give people options, so he and his team are always coming up with new ideas. Initially, Adam sourced his skis at yard sales or from acquaintance for very little. Today he has over seventy resources for his supplies, doing his part to keep old skis out of landfills.

As it is for many entrepreneurs, the road to success hasn't always been easy. His overhead is "mind-boggling," and includes trucks, trailers, and everything needed for production, including his brick and mortar show room. He typically works 60–70-hour weeks. "Working a 40-hour week feels like a vacation," he chuckles. He also admits there were times when he was inching close to bankruptcy. But prayer, ingenuity, and work ethic played a role in keeping his business afloat during those inevitable times of ebb and flow.

Experience helped as well. He had started other businesses in the past, but this one has proven different. "This one took off because I loved it," he shares. "Having an attitude of being grateful and staying humble is huge. Even when you're doing great, it's important not to get cocky."

It also helps to have a support and an accountability team of advisors around him to keep him honest. "I have a team of 6–8 people that I reach out to," he explains. "My mom has been an entrepreneur, and when my stepdad was alive, he was as well. I also turn to a couple of guys in the furniture business, a few MBA buddies, and some friends in the ski business."

For more information about Colorado Ski Furniture, visit: http://www.coloradoskichairs.com/

How to Get Started

Customize your ideas and business plan to your local market. If you live in Florida or Houghton Lake, Michigan, then salvaging water skis may be an interesting idea. If you live in Park City, Utah, then snow themes may work better. Other mountain locations may invite ideas that have already been successful, like art and furniture made from antlers, and canoe and oar themes. The L.L. Bean store in Lone Tree, Colorado, has a pair of canoe paddles as handles on the front doors—what a great idea! (As an example, check out Tippy Canoe at tippycanoedurango.com.)

Unique products like these are begging for an online presence. Be sure to build your audience online, especially using social media. Adam has over 47,000 followers on Facebook as of this writing!

Tips and Techniques for Building Your Business

Adam shares:

1. "Do something you're really stoked about. If you feel excited, it's going to help. Commit to going all in." Adam is a follower of Gary Vaynerchuk (Gary Vee), a renowned serial entrepreneur, and subscribes to the advice Gary shares in his books and podcasts.

2. "Work ridiculous amounts. I always put my sleep first, usually between 1:00 a.m. and 9:00 a.m. I'm getting eight hours."

3. Make sure you're offering something people really like.

4. Trust others, and get good advice.

5. Keep being inspired.

6. Respect your elders, and try to always learn.

Horizontal Growth

You can diversify your products and themes to sell to a wider audience, as Adam did, moving from Adirondack chairs to coffee tables and chairlift yard swings. Look for other outlets to reach more customers. Some entrepreneurs will begin by consigning their wares in other people's stores before eventually opening their own stores. This way, you are able to build scale and cash flow before you invest in your own storefront. You can have multiple consignment outlets as well. Next, you may want to shift your attention to online presence and sales.

Vertical Growth

By necessity, Adam has had to be creative about acquiring skis and other materials to produce furniture. As he claws his way up the supply chain, going to or creating sources for materials, he is experiencing vertical growth. He may decide to begin wholesaling to other stores as a way of growing his pipeline as well.

Variation

Business 23: *Junk Art*

From end tables and candleholders to a number of animal or human caricatures, if you've got a knack for welding and metal, combined with some artistic talent, there are people looking to buy your wares. You don't even need a brick-and-mortar building to sell these products. Etsy and eBay are just a couple of places to list your items. There is even a board game called Junk Art, where players are presented with junk and must create art from it. For inspiration, venture over to: https://www.pinterest.com/reneejmoore/scrap-metal-art/.

Business 24:
Repurposed Shipping Containers and Pallets

For as little as $1,000, you can buy a used shipping container and create a number of livable areas. Whether you want to put two together to create a tiny house, or use one for a man cave, she shed, office, guest room, workshop, garage, or hunting or fishing cabin, there is no limit to what you can recreate out of a simple steel structure that was once used to ship goods across land or water. Depending on how you design the structure, the retail price ranges from $30,000 to $70,000. (Check out https://customcontainerliving.com/.)

You can use old pallets to create doghouses, wall shelves, vertical planters, chandeliers, chairs, tables, room dividers, office furniture, and more. (For two successful businesses in the world of pallets, see http://www.knotty-pallet.com/, and, on Facebook, The Pallet Furniture.)

Resale Opportunities

Business 25: *Consignment and Thrift Selling*

You can start at fairs, neighborhood markets, flea markets, or farmer's markets, or from a storage unit. Consign your goods at someone else's consignment shop until you can afford your own. You also can sell certain items, such as cool furniture and jewelry, online. Check out the largest online consignment and thrift store, ThredUp.com. It gives a whole new meaning to the uniqueness of experienced clothing and accessories. To give you an idea of the potential, ThredUp just signed a massive partnership deal with Walmart.com, telegraphing to us what the future of retailing will look like—lots of choices in niche areas, including thrift! Look for lots of detail and how-to advice in the section "Online Selling."

Business 26: *Estate Sales*

You can jump into this opportunity with no cost by offering your services to clients who want to sell their belongings. This often happens after the death of a family member or prior to moving, when the family wants to sell most of their belongings. You hold yourself out as an estate sale facilitator, organizing, pricing, and spreading the word about sales by posting on social media. Over time, create an email list of prior and potential buyers, to whom you send announcements about upcoming sales. Build a digital database of consumers. This one is *sooo* easy.

You will promote the sale with flyers, email, and social media. You hold the sale, often Friday through Sunday, marking prices on the items, cashiering, and helping people load furniture into their cars and trucks. Your arrangement with the homeowner can be 35–45 percent of the proceeds. You've only invested your time.

5

Crafty Stuff:
Make It, Pin It, Sell It

All our dreams can come true,
if we have the courage to pursue them.
—WALT DISNEY

"Etsy is a global online marketplace, where people come together to make, sell, buy, and collect unique items," according to the company website. The site focuses on items handmade by the sellers. According to Statista, as of 2020, more than 4.4 million sellers sold goods through the Etsy platform, with over 39.4 million active buyers worldwide.

The sellers are the dreamers in our society, and they have the courage to make things happen. So do you.

There's money to be made by doing something you really love with all sorts of materials from the comfort of your home. The ideas are endless: you can make soap, you can knit garments and accessories, you can build birdhouses, and much more. Many have paved the way for you to join in the journey.

There are hundreds of business segments and ideas in this category. The ones in this chapter are listed because they are trending and very popular in the online sales universe, according to 2019 sales figures.

How to Get Started

As my team and I have heard over and over, a successful business sprouts from a good idea that is backed by passion. If you're lukewarm about your business venture, it's a sure bet it will flop quickly—if it ever gets off the ground in the first place. You don't want to be locked up in your woodworking shed making bird houses if you hate woodworking. Nor do you want to sit around all day knitting if you're allergic to yarn. Find something, as Danielle of Outlaw Soaps did, that reminds you to live your best life, one that serves others and bring joy to their lives.

In this age of Internet marketing, even with a brick-and-mortar business, a website and social media channels such as Facebook are essential for reaching your customer audience. Be sure to create a custom URL and user name that identifies your business.

Tips and Techniques for Building Your Business

Danielle and Russ believe in operating a values-based business. They espouse "The Magnificent Seven Outlaw Values" (https://liveoutlaw.com/pages/the-magnificent-seven-outlaw-values):

1. The *best* customer service
2. Incredible products
3. Ethical production
4. Kindness is king (and queen and all the other royalties)
5. Made in the U.S.A., supporting real people in local jobs
6. Responsible employers
7. Conscious commerce

Horizontal Growth

Horizontal growth is easy to develop in this business model by simply introducing additional related products, as Outlaw Soaps has done.

Vertical Growth

Outlaw Soaps experienced vertical growth by controlling more of its supply and distribution, making its own products, outsourcing some, and introducing a subscription gift box service.

I'm only going to name a few variations on the crafts theme here, because if I were to list every possibility, this book would be as long as *War and Peace*.

Business 27: *Pet Wellness and Grieving*

Another trending idea: grain-free, rawhide-free, healthy items for pets.

Another idea on a similar theme: a gift box with a succulent plant, candle, and sympathy card to commemorate the loss of a pet. It recently sold nearly 4,000 units for just under $20. That's almost $80,000 in sales for just one item on Etsy.

Business 28: *Athleisure*

Custom tanks, leggings, and water bottles are easy to source and continue to grow in popularity at both traditional and online retailers. (Lululemon, a retailer who sells such items, is posting big gains this year). You can source print-on-demand products if you don't want to make them yourself, so once again you can take custom orders online with little up-front investment. The three items I mentioned above are easy to source as custom products. Put your special designs on these items, and sell them as your own brand (see Print On Demand (POD) in Business 83 on page 180, and drop shipping in the Guide to Website, Online Store, and Virtual Office Tools on page 235).

Business 29: *Farmhouse Signs*

It's not a new idea, but this is still a strong seller. If you can make your signs look authentic and do custom orders, you may find a good clientele.

Business 30: *Steel Pipe and Industrial-Themed Furniture*

In style for younger buyers! If you know how to make these items already, you don't need my help in manufacturing. You will use the retail outlets that I describe in chapters 18 and 19 to sell and promote your creations.

Business 31: *Accessory Bags and Utility Aprons*

Craft Booth.com says, "Bags that go over walkers, custom bags that have pouches that fit phones, and even utility aprons with pockets for crafting etc., are quite popular. Among creatives in particular—bags that have pockets for specific things like hooks/needles, etc. If you can customize it to fit a need and be both pretty and practical, it's a bonus."

If you need any more inspiration, head over to Pinterest, and search for "crafts to sell." If you love the soap story, read about another soap entrepreneur by researching Dr. Bronner's Magic Soaps, DrBronner.com.

Emanuel Bronner's story is one of the most bizarre entrepreneurial stories I know. He fled the Germany in 1928, eventually losing his remaining family to the Holocaust. After escaping from a mental institution in 1945, he became a traveling preacher who gave away soap at his events, as he preached his own his holistic, "All-in-One" philosophy. He soon realized people were coming for the free soap rather than the message so he began printing his messages, rather long ones, on the soap bottles. Today, his grandsons run the multi-million-dollar business, with grandson David serving as CEO (Cosmic Engagement Officer)."

6

Local Lessons

*Teachers have three loves: love of learning, love of learners,
and the love of bringing the first two loves together.*
—SCOTT HAYDEN, AMERICAN COMPOSER OF RAGTIME MUSIC

There are so many variations on this theme that we will only focus on a few in this chapter; however, the business models and business plans are similar for most of the coaching and teaching market segments. The key to success is to build from your strength—a skill or knowledge base that you already have or that you can learn quickly.

Business 32: *Sand Castle Lessons*

With a tagline of "We Don't Do Boring," Andy Hancock believes his job—and the job of his team of professional artists—is to give families better vacations by helping them build the best sandcastles ever.

Born in Melbourne, Australia, Andy arrived in South Padre Island, Texas, in 2002, by way of the United Kingdom, after meeting an American sand sculptor carving ice in Finland. He began Sand Castle Lessons after seeing how sandcastles were being built and how customers were treated. "I thought I could make customers happier and more comfortable."

And so he has. Two-hour group lessons start at $295, three-hour lessons go for $395, and the VIP package with Andy, who has won the American championship for sand castle building thirteen out of fourteen years, is a day-long event, costing $1,200 for a group.

Andy's fifteen-plus year journey has been quite a ride. It includes building a replica of the Alamo with 300 tons of sand—the biggest sand sculpture ever—on a beach in Texas and having a customer come 2,500 miles just to have a lesson with him.

He's had some challenging moments as well, including overcoming local negativity to new ideas. However, by partnering with local business and providing space on his website to highlight other services in and around South Padre Island, he not only became accepted but successfully marketed his business.

Andy believes that a business like his can be built with lifelong experience, and not necessarily in your current field of choice. One thing about starting a business, according to Andy: "All of your previous experience in *anything* counts." And he should know. He's been a motorcycle engineer, insurance broker, factory worker, and wood and sand sculptor, and has held a bevy of other temp jobs.

Andy shares lessons on his YouTube channel (with over 14,000 subscribers), passing on the science of how to make a better sandcastle. The company also has a line of tools, with kits ranging from $33 to $130. They even offer rentals of trash cans, shovels, and other tools from $40 to $100 per day.

A day with Andy and his crew is complete with everything needed for families and friends to dive into their creations. All Andy asks is that "You supply the smiles." Search for Sand Castle Lessons with the hashtag #howtobuildasandcastle, or visit Andy's website: www.sandcastlelessons.com.

His YouTube Channel is https://www.youtube.com/channel/UChFFnw4EU_26F6SWiAR6ZUg.

Tips and Techniques for Building Your Business

Andy's advice for readers:

- It's a lot of hard work, with long hours and most of all, lots of smiling!
- Be the best at what you do, regardless of what it is.
- Treat others the way you would like to be treated, so they go away and say, "Wow! You have to do this!" to others.

Horizontal Growth

Horizontal growth can come in different forms. You will customarily seek to sell more or different services to more people. Andy might set up at different locations, partner with other tourist-oriented businesses in his area to attract more clients, or offer different type of creative classes. I've known Andy for many years and discovered he is a terrific chainsaw artist as well! He creates amazing sculptures from logs with a chainsaw. He could leverage his reputation as a sculptor of sand to market himself a sculptor of wood. This is such a nichey business that he wouldn't have to worry about many competitors. I could only find about a dozen chainsaw sculptors with an online presence worldwide.

There may be some safety challenges to teaching students with a live chainsaw, so perhaps a subscription plan sold to aspiring sculptors would be a way to marry this art with the digital age. I would post basic how-to videos on Facebook and YouTube for free, build an audience, and follow up by offering a subscription (maybe $19–$29 per month) providing more advanced classes, equipment analysis and recommendations, and videos, with downloadable patterns. You could distinguish yourself by featuring great camera angles and close-ups.

Vertical Growth

One way that Andy is exploring vertical growth is by selling sand-castle building kits, bags, and supplies. Aspiring masters can buy a variety of sandcastle building tools or toolkits from him. From my memory of sunny days on the beach with Andy, his most popular accessory package is an attractive beach bag full of fun and useful tools and accessories.

A sandcastle instructor could also tap into vertical growth by offer package trips to out-of-towners. People often travel a long way to take lessons from Andy. He could offer a lodging/meal/lesson plan at an attractive markup and experience vertical growth as he taps into the market for sandcastle tourism. You can easily obtain discounted room and meal vouchers from local hotels and restaurants and put them in your all-inclusive trip package.

Business 33: *Fitness*

Share your love of karate, kickboxing, fitness, surfing, yoga, or dance. The world is chock-full of one-on-one instructors and trainers in every variety of sport, dance, and fitness, so you need to differentiate yourself. I have friends in almost every segment of instruction from surfing to personal fitness trainers, and I only know two that make a good living at it. One is a former NFL football player, who is able to keep a full schedule for fifty weeks a year, and a couples intimacy coach. If you have been a professional athlete, you can leverage your celebrity into a full-time training gig, although I would posit that you should have more lucrative ways to leverage it than personal training or starting a gym.

Although offering personal lessons in sport, fitness, or dance is a way to start a business instantly, in itself it isn't likely to offer a robust income, because in common disciplines, you have serious competition. There are not many sandcastle master artists in the world, but there are millions of Zumba instructors.

So how do you use your skill in sport, art, or fitness as a stepping-stone to a bigger, more lucrative business? First, follow the subscription model, which I've laid out several times in this book. Build an audience and then sell subscriptions for higher value training, videos, and collateral material.

Another way is to find a niche that has less competition. Yoga, for example, has its roots in Eastern mysticism, which is not appealing to everyone. What if you offered Christian yoga exercise classes? When Brooke Boon, an experienced yogi, came to Christian faith, she stopped doing yoga but found that what she now calls "praise moves" helped her draw closer to God while staying fit, and Holy Yoga was born (https://holyyoga.net/about/team/). Brook is not only the founder of Holy Yoga but also the creator of their instructor training programs and author of *Holy Yoga: Exercise for the Christian Body and Soul* and coauthor of *Hatha Yoga Illustrated*.

Organizations like Holy Yoga provide training for first-time instructors as well as experienced instructors. With 2.3 billion Christians worldwide, Christianity is by far the world's largest religion, yet there are only a few thousand instructors of this practice in three or four networks (Holy Yoga, Christian Yoga Association, Yoga Faith, and others). There is still a huge unmet need for you to explore if Christian faith and yoga are part of your life. If I were starting this business, I'd experiment with live online Zoom classes.

Business 34: *Art*

Whether you're interested in painting, landscape design, scrapbooking, events pairing wine and painting, or other such activities, there is an audience waiting for you. Scrapbooking and stamping classes are ubiquitous, so I won't dive into much detail here. You can find plenty of resources at StampingImperfection.com and Scrapbook.com.

One of the more fascinating trends I've observed is the growth in themed art classes or events. Owler, a website that tracks various industries, ranks Painting with a Twist as number one in this space, with Paint Nite, Pinot's Palette, Wine & Design, and Koncept Events rounding out the top five. Painting with a Twist is a franchise, so it doesn't fit our business model in this book, but all five of these companies can offer inspiration and a business template that you can modify to your individual taste.

Canvas & Cocktails' name belies its family-friendly offerings. They have everything from Kid Camp, private themed parties, Canvas Kids, Doggy and Me theme nights (paint with your dog, using pawprints aa flowers), to company events. They pivoted to Zoom classes in the post-Covid period.

Interestingly, I've also been hosting Zoom events, and sending GrubHub gift certificates to participants with some success. We still share the event and food—virtually!

I've followed a few friends who have begun similar classes with good success, but not with enough frequency to make sustainable businesses. The key to growth is to host a variety of classes with different themes and throw in art-themed birthday parties and corporate events. You'll provide the canvases, paint, easels, and brushes as well as a lesson, usually with everyone painting the same subject.

This business is easy to promote on social media, because you'll have great photos and videos of people having fun and taking home their very own masterpieces.

Business 35: *Horses, Dogs and More*

Whether it's equestrian riding and handling or behavior lessons for dogs and their owners, folks love their animals. Share your animal whispering talents with this crowd. Again, it's important to find an unmet need or a niche.

Animal massage and bodywork. Why not get paid to pet dogs? Pet massage therapy is a real thing now. In the United States, charges range from $35 to $50 per half-hour or hour session. This is a nascent industry, with only eleven educational providers in the United States and four in Europe. There are only about 400 professional members of the International Association of Animal Massage & Bodywork/Association of Canine Water Therapy. With 470 million dogs, 370 million cats, and 60 million horses worldwide, there are opportunities to participate in an emerging industry.

About half of the world's horse population is in the Americas—about a third in North America.

There are still many unknown variables in this business, such as the extent of demand and licensing requirements. Some states only allow veterinarians to perform massage therapy, some require the supervision of a veterinarian, and some, like Montana, have no requirements. Go to https://iaamb.org/resources/laws-by-state/ for a list of laws by state. In the United Kingdom, you can learn how to become a canine massage therapist at K9-Massage.co.uk. Geraldine Paradis has a fascinating equine massage and bodywork practice in France; check her out at Naturolistic.com.

Animal training. The demand for animal trainers is expected to grow by 60 percent over the next few years, according to Recruiter. com, with California being the most crowded market. Animal training and lessons can take many forms and may include training the beast or the boss! Horse trainers often train the client's horse when the owner is not present but also give riding lessons to the owner, so you're training both the horse and the rider. Training is sometimes combined with boarding and can range from $300 to $1,000 per month and more for a well-known trainer. If you're starting out and don't have stalls to rent, then partner with a stable or barn where you can train horses and give riding lessons.

In the smaller pet space, you have many options. Before investing in kennels and such, try offering "Obedience Boot Camp" on a Saturday and test the market. If you develop a following, you can grow your business into more regular classes, and leverage online lessons into a subscription model. Eventually you may grow into having a boarding school or stable.

As with all these business ideas, start small and find some success, and build a cool social media presence with fun photos of successful results with animals and owners. You can start with a one-page website that you set up on WordPress or a similar site without paying big bucks to a web designer. You don't need a deep, multipage website in the early days of your new business. Use the templates available in WordPress, and just let your web page reflect you. It doesn't require tons of graphic art and design at first. Use your photos and videos. Ignore the design elements and focus on creating good content in your blog and social media. If you're teaching dressage, show pictures and videos of you or your students doing well. If you're training dogs, show pictures and videos of happy owners and cute pets finding the magic of mutual respect and a healthy relationship. Many people crave a good relationship with their furry friends and freedom from the dysfunction that is too often found in pet families. You're not just selling training; you're selling peace and harmony; remember that when you're posting your images and videos. You can post short, smart success technique videos, then invite people to classes or to subscribe to your service. A monthly subscription might include in-depth training videos and one in-person coaching session per quarter.

Business 36:
Driver Education and Certification Training

Make yourself stand out as a driver's ed instructor by adopting a theme, such as comedy driver education. Once you grow the business into a storefront, put your school next to the DMV. I met Art Benavides when he was a young, hardworking entrepreneur in 1994. He had a photography business and was teaching driver's education and defensive driving classes, following in his father's footsteps. Today, the Benavides Driving School (www.benavides drivingschool.net) teaches dozens of different types of classes from three locations, including a variety of court-mandated classes, such as theft, truancy, and parenting classes in addition to traditional driving classes, which include new driver education, defensive driving, and road driving tests.

When I needed to take a defensive driving course to get a traffic ticket deferred, I looked up Art. It turned out he had added his own personal touch to the defensive driving course, telling jokes and interspersing the required material with skits and funny routines. I had been dreading the loss of an entire day to the course, but once we got started, it was fun, and the time flew by. A comedy driving school is a great entrée to other valuable education services, which can help you grow horizontally.

There is no standardized training requirement for becoming a driver's education instructor. You will need a high-school diploma or GED, go through your state's driver instructor training program if required, and have a valid driver's license. According to Payscale .com, the average income for driver's ed teachers is $45,826. You can start without a building by advertising online and holding your periodic classes in a rented space. Once you have built up some cash flow, you can consider a permanent space. With today's sudden increase in criminal activity, court-mandated trainings and classes may be a growing segment of the private pay education market.

In addition to driver education and court-mandated classes, a cottage industry has been built around certification training. In most states, if you're going to be an insurance agent or stockbroker (general securities representative), you may want to take a privately offered training class before tackling the big test to obtain a license.

Most classes require the instructor to be certified, so you will need to take your own training and pass a certification test. Many instructors obtain certification in fields in which they have acquired experience in the past. My wife needed to be certified in cardiopulmonary resuscitation (CPR) for her business. She continued taking courses until she became a certified CPR educator/trainer. Former stockbrokers and insurance agents often enjoy teaching courses on those subjects. Some publishers operate a franchise model, such as Sylvan Learning. The franchiser fully prepares the entrepreneur to host classes and proctor tests.

In Texas, if you are going to be a server, seller, or manager of an entity licensed by the Texas Alcoholic Beverage Commission (TABC), you need to be TABC certified. One comedy driving school, ComedyDefensiveDriving.com, has also spun off Comedy TABC.com. If you've got to be certified, why not have fun while learning? Education (excluding primary and secondary education) is big business.

Business 37: *Language Lessons*

Are you fluent in another language? Offer private tutoring, group lessons, online lessons, and subscriptions.

Even with her degree in business, Lisa Walter slowly realized while working at her nine-to-five office job that she was missing something. "Reflecting back on my work history, I came to the conclusion that I truly missed working with children and that I was damn good at it," she shares. "After racking my brain on what I could do to harmonize my current office job and work with children again, I came up with the idea to tutor students in German after hours."

Lisa had enough connections and a great network, so she decided to post an ad on the Facebook Community page for a German immersion school to see how the idea of tutoring would be perceived. It took time to build, but her idea proved valuable.

"I started with only three students, and within two years have built up my reputation to help eighteen students with their German," Lisa says. "My tutoring gig kept me afloat while I was on maternity leave and continues to supplement my income now that I've gone back to work in a part-time teaching position."

Lisa knew her business would succeed when she began receiving random text messages or calls from families that heard about her from other families. They had seen evidence of their children's success while working with her.

Lisa has had challenges, mainly revolving around inconsistent cash flow—something many entrepreneurs echo. However, she's adjusted, and her business continues to grow.

Initially, Lisa was charging $25 per hour for her services. Now her rate is $40 per hour, and she has a waiting list. Word is out on how successful she is at tutoring.

In addition to enabling them to learn a second language, Lisa makes her work with children fun. "I believe that each and every one of my students love coming to me for tutoring, something that I take major pride in," she says. "I make it fun enough for them to not realize we are putting in some work to get those grades up."

See chapter 13, which goes more into the world of virtual teaching.

7

Specialty Tours

*Twenty years from now, you will be more disappointed by the things
you didn't do than by the ones you did do. So throw off the bowlines.
Catch the trade winds in your sails. Explore. Dream. Discover.*
—MARK TWAIN

Most of us love to explore new horizons. Most of us are meant to
be wanderers and adventurers. It sparks life in our souls. Here are a
few ideas for turning the mundane into the magical and providing
experiences in your own backyard.

Innovative Tourism Ideas

I love business ideas that are novel—sometimes just for the sheer
creativity, but more importantly because uniqueness equals nicheness, and nicheness equals loyal customers that stick to you. It also
means you may find less competition for your new business, because
you're not doing the same thing that everyone else is doing.

The travel and tourism industry is changing rapidly. Today
many people are seeking an experience rather than just a destination. This demand is driving a proliferation of novel travel ideas and
curated experiences, from cruises that feature celebrities to destina-

tion trips that feature an immersive experience, such as traveling to Italy to attend cooking classes.

Immersive Travel and Curated Experiences

According to Prachi Joshi, writing for the Live Mint website, the experiential categories, such as food tours and cooking classes, has grown at annual rates from 50 to 125 percent. Online travel aggregators (OTAs) are ramping up their offerings of unique tours and activities. The good news for you is that most of these curated experiences happen locally, at the grassroots level. Here's where you come in, creating, hosting, or organizing the experience in a location or area in which you have expertise or interest. Go to Airbnb's home page, and you will find four business lines at the top: Short-Term Stays, Long-Term Stays, Experiences, and Online Experiences (the latter is new post-Covid).

I recently discovered a literary online adventure—"Follow a Plague Doctor through Prague." "Through video, we'll follow the footsteps of Dr. Alexander Schamsky, an unknown Czech hero who fought the plague in 1713," write Airbnb hosts Lucie and David. With an investment of $17 per person, participants will be guided through the history of the "hidden jewels of Old Town Prague." The couple offers this virtual experience in English and German (https://www.airbnb.com/experiences/1658926).

Airbnb has taken over the world. It is not only the biggest OTA, but it is bigger than the top five hotel brands combined. The point is this: if the biggest player in travel is betting half the company on experiences and curated travel, then this is likely a well-established trend that needs people like you to make it work. Curated travel needs hosts, and if you have a particular skill, interest, or local knowledge then you can host innovative travel. What's great about this idea is that you don't need a residence or hotel to rent out. A curated experience may place a guest at the home of one host while having their adventure with the experience host. This segment of businesses is so much fun. Here are a few of my favorites:

Business 38: *Spring Break Tours*

Inertia Tours (https://www.inertiatours.com/) provides spring break destination packages to college students. Their primary destinations are South Padre Island, Texas; Panama City, Florida; and Breckenridge, Colorado. The packages provide students with the whole spring break experience, including party condos, meals, pool parties, night events, concerts, and party cruises. The staff provides concierge service throughout the trip. Chad Hart's company is pure genius: his niche is so narrow that he dominates his business sector. His planners work with fraternities, sororities, clubs, and affinity groups nearly a year ahead of spring break and bring them to the destinations as groups. Inertia's spring break operation is massive, hosting thousands of students over a three- to four-week period each year. Chad buys rooms at hotels and condos in blocks, which, like an air traffic controller, he allocates to the incoming groups.

Business 39: *Themed Tours*

Curated experiences revolving around customers' interests or hobbies are on the rise. Interests may include food, philanthropy, history, fitness, triathlon training, race destination, fashion and fabric, meditation, or simply an over-the-top VIP or concierge experience. There are hundreds of viable themes. Here are four themes that I like.

Business 40: *Holy Land Tour*

Brad and Jeanie Brough (https://www.baptists4israel.com/about-us/ faculty-and-staff) run a variety of programs in the Holy Land, including programs that range from seminars and internships to undergraduate and graduate programs. These are technically educational programs rather than tourism trips. The trip that Cheri and I took included archeological sites but morphed, at our request, into a quasi-adventure trip. We hiked along the headwaters of the Jordan River in the mountainous north and to the top of Mount Sinai and Masada, camped in the Negev Desert, and spent a morning crewing on a commercial fishing boat on the Sea of Galilee. This was in addition to visiting many well-known and historically significant sites. This was an extraordinary and memorable trip. If you have expertise or familiarity with a destination or you just know your way around your home turf, you might be able to create extraordinary experiences for guests.

Business 41: *The Italian Pasta Experience*

Nonna Nerina (https://news.airbnb.com/nonna-nerina-welcomes -travelers-to-the-roman-countryside-to-learn-more-about-italian -pasta-tradition/) is an eighty-four-year-old experience host on Airbnb. She lives in Palombara Sabina, near Rome, and hosts handmade pasta making experiences on Airbnb with the help of her granddaughter, Chiara. Guests walk the medieval streets of the village to a kitchen in the old winepress in Nerina's home, where she teaches them the how to make pasta from scratch. Hundreds of people from all over the world have traveled to the Roman countryside to roll gnocchi with Nerina. During the Covid quarantine, Chiara posted experiences online.

This has got to be one of my all-time favorite business ideas. It has everything you could want in a business—it's international, it attracts multigenerational participation, and there's a nonna!

Think about your special talent or interest, take a tour on Airbnb Experiences for additional inspiration, and start planning your specialty tour or experience.

Business 42: *Private Tours*

Recently Cheri and I traveled to Israel to visit friends near Haifa. We met a fascinating couple, who knew everything about Israel and escorted us to various points of interest and historical sites. No tickets, no lines, no hurrying through historical sites to get back to the bus. We saw everything! Places we would never have found in a brochure or on the Internet, and intimate experiences we were unlikely to have had in a big group. We prayed at Christ's empty tomb and sang hymns a capella in Christ Church, whose altar bears my son's middle name, Emmanuel.

If you know your way around, this business has low barriers to entry. You can find resources online to learn more about joining a professional guide association and to list your availability: PrivateTour.com, ToursByLocals.com, PrivateGuide.com, and LocalGuiding.com. In Britain, the British Guild of Tourist Guides grants certain guides the Blue Badge, which, they claim, is the U.K.'s highest guide qualification. Be sure to check your locale's licensing or registration requirements.

Business 43: *Bicycle Adventures*

My wife, Cheri, trained for triathlon with a great group of friends now known as the Gator Chasers (because they do their open water swims in alligator-infested waters). Bob and Arlene (both in their sixties) are part of the original five or six athletes. As they began to explore their sport, they picked up a tandem bike and were always easy to spot at races—sometimes theirs was the only tandem present. They were having a blast as they approached retirement and were full of more verve than most of our friends in their thirties. Eventually they added destination races (bicycle, duathlon, and triathlon) to their itinerary, as well as guided bicycle tours. The last trip they told me about was a bicycle tour of Ireland (https://cycle holidaysire.land/). They were atwitter as they described the roads, scenery, food, pubs, and inns. John Hagney, their guide, knew the history and, they said, was also very funny. I started thinking about what a great business model bicycle tours could be for an aspiring entrepreneur. You could offer tours in thousands of different destinations: self-guided, with or without a SAG (support and gear) vehicle. Your guest can ride from inn to inn, or you could offer camping tours. The adventure combinations are endless.

Green Marble Tours (https://www.greenmarblecycletours .com/guided-cycling-tours/) was founded by Wilma Heim, a German expatriate, and offers a variety of bike tours of Ireland, from self-guided to custom tours. They provide hybrid, road, tandem, and e-bikes. Guests ride at their own pace and can hitch a ride in the SAG if they've had enough for the day. Stops include historical sites, cheese makers, salmon smokehouses, and whiskey distilleries. The day ends in quaint country inns or small hotels with your suitcase waiting for you. If you love cycling, this is a great business idea that you can start on a small scale. Rent your family's bikes, plan the route in the locations you know best, and provide VIP service to your adventurers.

Business 44: *Travel by Motorcycle*

Helge Pederson, a photographer and the author of *Ten Years on Two Wheels*, completed an epic solo motorcycle ride around the world, spanning 250,000 miles and seventy-seven countries. Helge's experiences have been featured in *National Geographic, Time,* and *The New York Times* as well as on *PBS* and the Discovery Channel. In 2000, he launched a GlobeRiders World Tour (http://www.globeriders .com/), where he guided fourteen riders from Tokyo to Munich. Since that initial journey GlobeRiders, has been conducting tours across the globe. The trip in 2021 was Cape Town to Cairo, a 15,000-kilometer, sixty-four-day riding exploit across the African continent. As Helge's website says, it's "the last great adventure."

My neighbor participated in the China to Munich trip. It was the epic adventure of a lifetime. He told me his stories in wide-eyed wonder. Not only is a company like GlobeRiders a great business, it is opening the world to people who would never be able to plan a trip like this on their own. This hints of doing good while doing well.

While you would need considerable skills and experience to facilitate transcontinental tours, there are a myriad of possibilities in local or regional tours. My cousin Al, an antique motorcycle enthusiast since the sixties, executed trips from Canada to South America with great success and no prior experience. (I'm not saying you should aim for South America on your first trip, just that it is doable.) If you lived near the Pacific Coast Highway, you could host a tour on that route. Other popular routes are:

- Tail of the Dragon, winding along US 129 in western North Carolina, eastern Tennessee, and north Georgia

- Twisted Sisters in Texas, along three Hill Country ranch roads, 335, 336 and 337
- The Blue Ridge Parkway from Virginia to North Carolina
- Skyline Drive in Virginia's Shenandoah National Park
- The Going-to-the-Sun Road in Montana's Glacier National Park

A Napa Valley tour, anybody? The possibilities are almost endless. Everybody lives somewhere, and maybe where you live is of interest to others. I could imagine a cool tour through the Everglades to Southmost Point in Key West (not in summer—mosquitos!). How about a Chesapeake Bay tour? The Eastern Shore has tons of great stops, inns, and food, and the Chesapeake Bay Bridge-Tunnel is one of the engineering wonders of the world. It's twenty-three miles long, with a 90,000-foot span in the middle, and a good portion of it is out of sight of land. You're literally driving across the sea. What a rush on a motorcycle! Take your love of motorcycles to new heights.

Most customers will want to ride their own motorcycles and will trailer or ride to your starting point. If you are going to provide motorcycles, begin by renting your family's bikes, or sublease from a local operator until you've generated enough cash flow to purchase bikes and trikes to rent.

I think there is a subniche in trike tours for seniors, if you want to explore that opportunity. Seniors are more inclined to purchase a tour and to appreciate support than, say, an amped-up thirty-year-old. Look for more tips below.

How to Get Started

Research your competitors. You can learn a lot from them. Take a tour with them! You'll learn most of what you need to know.

Who is your target audience? Once you identify your ideal client profile, it becomes easier to market to them. Think of the client niches we explored in this chapter: bicyclists, motorcyclists, fishing enthusiasts, foodies, Holy Land pilgrims, and spring breakers. What other readily identifiable audiences are out there? IntrepidTravel.com (https://www.intrepidtravel.com/us/theme/retreats) identifies these categories:

- **18–29s.** For socially conscious folks who want to travel with a group their own age and have authentic experiences while making a difference along the way
- **Active adventures,** from trekking and snorkeling to higher-octane experiences, like biking in Madagascar or whitewater rafting in the Amazon
- **Adventure cruising.** If you already own a boat, perhaps you could host trips on a site like Louisiana's Lake Pontchartrain or up the Mississippi. What's your locale like?
- **Cycling.** Covered above
- **Expeditions** to wild places
- **Family trips** with activities for all ages
- **Festivals.** If you live in New Orleans or near any big festival or bowl game, why not host a weekend on that theme?
- **Food themes,** such as street fare, urban, and or cultural food experiences
- **Lonely Planet experiences.** For intrepid visitors who want to get to the core of a destination, with insights from local leaders
- **Winter trips.** If snowshoeing, cross-country skiing, or snow-mobiling is your thing, you may be able to host visitors to a great experience.
- **Sailing.** Got a sailboat? Take people on sunset cruises and make a killing. Check out sailspi.com.

- **Short breaks**. From an overnight backpack to a weekend in your lake house. Short-term breaks are big bucks.
- **Urban adventures**. If you live in a big city, you bring knowledge to the enterprise. Get creative. Popular New York City tours, for example, are New York Catacombs by Candlelight, Ghost Tour of Greenwich Village, Underground Tour of NYC Subway, and Flatiron Food-Architecture-History Tour. In San Francisco, one couple does a Love Tour in a 1968 Peter Max–inspired VW microbus (https://www.viator.com/tours/San-Francisco/San-Francisco-Love-Tour/d651-23068P2).
- **Walking and trekking**. Walking tours are some of the most straightforward businesses you can start. Combine your local knowledge with a pair of sneakers, and you're ready to go!
- **Wildlife**. I lived on South Padre Island, Texas, for many years. It's a birding and butterfly destination ripe for hosted birding experiences. It is home to more bird species than anywhere else in the United States.

Marketing

Websites and social media. As with most businesses, your digital image has got to be on point, using the techniques I've shared in other sections. In addition, look for ways to feature your adventures and experiences on social media. A good example is the GlobeRiders YouTube channel (https://www.youtube.com/user/GlobeRidersLLC).

The first time I visited it and watched them riding the Silk Road from Turkey to China, I was hooked! I even started shopping for a motorcycle (what was I thinking?). Remember, it's how you make people feel that differentiates you from the crowd. Their videos give me FOMO (fear of missing out). Can your prospects visualize themselves free and on the open road? Whatever experience you're offering, make it look cool on Instagram, YouTube, and Facebook. Post pictures and videos that draw people in.

Networks and groups. In addition to Airbnb experiences, there are many other websites and groups you can join to list your specialty tour or experience, like the online resources I listed earlier (PrivateTour.com, ToursByLocals.com, PrivateGuide.com, and LocalGuiding.com). You can find others related to your specific niche. As an example, you can partner with TripAdvisor.com to sell your tours, activities, and promote your business to millions of travelers worldwide at this site: https://supplier.viator.com/sign-up -info?m=62034&localeCode=.

If bicycle tours are going to be your jam, you will also want to embed yourself into the cycling community through online groups, cycle shops, and similar venues.

Tips and Techniques for Building Your Business

You are the destination in most of the business ideas I'm showing you in this chapter. It takes experience and money to host travels abroad, but you may already be an expert at something in your hometown. Build from strength—showcase your special talent or knowledge on your home-turf first, then expand your business.

Use what you have in inventory. In order to start your business with little or no money, take inventory. What do you bring to the project? Talent, knowledge, or just proximity to something cool? Begin there and build on it. Once you have adequate cash flow from your business, you can expand into more ambitious offerings.

Licenses and permits. These ideas and models have fairly uncomplicated steps to get started, but in many locations, you will need a license and/or permit, so be sure you check with the local authorities for the necessary requirements. Don't skip this step—I know one guide who was a repeat offender for guiding without a license, and he served jail time for it. *¡Cuidado!*

Risks. One of my associates participated in a motorcycle trip from Texas to Tierra del Fuego, at the tip of South America. Within the first hour of the trip, the group made it across the US–Mexico border. At the first red light in Mexico, one of their riders was run over and fatally wounded by a five-ton truck. Travel, especially adventure travel, entails risk. Cheri and I have been on several trips where participants fell ill or were injured. These are real risks, which should be managed by mitigation and insurance. In addition to licensing requirements, be sure to understand any bonding and insurance requirements that may pertain to your business idea.

Copycat. It's OK to copy a great idea from another town, but it can be fatal to copy your neighbor's successful business idea. Don't be a copycat in your community unless you absolutely, positively know you can defeat the business you're copying. If everyone in your town is doing snowshoe treks, find something different or unique. Don't hang your shingle in a crowded marketplace. Experiences like those offered by Airbnb are newish and still have a lot of upside potential, but specialty tours are not new. Hence there may be many competitors, so be careful to not simply copy what you see in your community. You've got to be unique if you're going to stand out and attract customers. Example: I spend a fair amount of time around the water, and there is no end to the number of entrepreneurs that want to be in the jet ski rental business. I suppose somebody is making money at it, but I've never met them. I even coached a few over the years, but none survived. Like kayak and small-sail rentals, it's a crowded and seasonal space. If you make a jet boat contract with a big resort, you might have something worthwhile. Otherwise look for uniqueness and a segment you can carve out as your own. In my opinion, a romantic sunset gourmet dinner cruise on a sailboat has much better odds at success and would be more profitable than just renting equipment to passers-by. Study the experiences community that is building around Airbnb, Trip Advisor, and others. I think this segment has a long growth curve ahead of it, and you can more easily distinguish yourself in this forum.

Go and start your business today! High adventure awaits you.

Horizontal Growth

Obvious horizontal growth strategies would include expanding locations, destinations, and varying experiences in each location.

Vertical Growth

The vertical growth strategies for this business model will be a bit more complex. They include things like online listings, growing those to include others (hosting other adventure hosts), and then creating a marketplace for the experiences and destinations. You can also act as a behind-the-scenes wholesaler of destinations and experiences in a cloud-based program that can distribute vacancies and booking capabilities to multiple retailers. You would in essence link the provider with resellers domestically or around the world. This is an already established business model.

Variations

Business 45: *Celebrity Host*

Add a celebrity or specialist to the experience or tour. These are sometimes called "hosted tours." Here is an example: as you may have figured out by now, I love fly-fishing, and I've found all-inclusive fishing trips where a well-known fisherperson or guide will participate, enjoying meals with clients and usually offering a couple of short sessions on topics like casting or equipment selection. These celebrities may be people who have had a television show on a relevant topic, well-known bloggers, or Instagram celebrities. All of these will attract clients and will often allow you to charge a little extra for the privilege of rubbing elbows with the celebrity or specialist. Your rate structure will include the specialist's fee and an extra margin for you.

Flip Pallot (flippallot.com), host of *The Walker Cay Chronicles* television show, among others, is the author of several books, an inventor, and well-known adventurer. I became acquainted with him a few years ago and joined him for a killer trip—fly-fishing for blue marlin off the coast of Abacos, Bahamas. It was fun, unique, and on the edge of fly-fishing possibilities: catching blue water fish on a fly rod using a teaser technique developed by Flip. Priceless!

What's your niche? Is it food, history, wine, your city, a sport, the national park in your backyard? Open your mind to the possibilities.

Look for additional sector-specific resources online to learn more, or check out the book *Start Your Own Travel Business* by Rich Mentzer.

8

Mi Casa, Su Casa

The secret of success is to do the common thing
uncommonly well.

—JOHN D. ROCKEFELLER JR.

Opening your home to strangers isn't for everyone, but if you have idle assets on your hand—a room, or maybe three or four—renting part of your house may be an opportunity for you. This could mean long-term rentals or shorter terms ones using Airbnb, Vacation Rental by Owner (VRBO), or Evolve Vacation Rental.

Even if you don't have space of your own to rent, you could offer your management services to someone who does. Let's explore your options.

Business 46: *Charlotte Community Rentals*

Jason Wallace hadn't really intended to build a business out of sharing his home with others. However, that's exactly what happened. Jason bought a house in Charlotte, North Carolina, where he lived with his then girlfriend. They only used the first floor, so Jason had the idea of renting out the idle space.

"I said to her, 'We have this idle asset, and we never go upstairs. Why don't we rent out a bedroom or two and make some extra money?'" Jason says. "She was vehemently opposed to it."

Six months later, the couple broke up, and Jason posted an ad the day after she moved out. "The first lesson in life is to align yourself with someone who believes in your dreams. Since then, every girlfriend gets it," he adds.

By day, Jason worked in the financial industry, and before long (and an additional house or two later), he saw that he was on to something, so he gave up his day job and began creating a life out of building his business—Charlotte Community Rentals. Today Jason owns thirteen houses, where five or six people share space with one another, and Jason oversees the operations from his original coliving residence. His houses fill up almost as quickly as he buys them, so he has rental income pouring in even before the first payment is due.

Experiment Until You Get It Right

Through some trial and error, Jason learned that he needed to target the right people to live in his houses. He identified these individuals as professionals who work from nine-to-five, who do not work at home, and whom he'd enjoy hanging out with at night.

"I refined my description of the people I want in my houses as driven, purposeful people who go to work and make it happen. I found that people who are driven and purposeful recognize the value of aligning themselves with other driven professionals," he explains.

Knowing whom he wanted to attract as coliving residents, Jason began listening for key signs of the right fit as early as the initial showing of the property, essentially conducting an informal interview: who doesn't fit? Those he's decided should look elsewhere include someone who has just broken up with their partner and is desperate to find another place to live, as well as the professional who works ten-hour days and spends evenings and weekends playing video games. However, professionals who are "crushing it" during the day and engaging in adventurous activities on weekends are the perfect match.

"Driven people have driven lives," he says. "About halfway through my second house and every house since then, I have a process that I use to interview potential residents. It's formulaic, even down to the same jokes."

The residents of Charlotte Community Rentals are diverse. Men and women share space, as well as blue-collar and white-collar workers, along with people from different countries. His well-refined concept is simple: to provide a housing alternative for purposeful, driven people who appreciate spending time with quality professionals. His secret to success is finding quality people with goals and ambitions. Well steeped in the high-performance world, having trained with Brendon Burchard and Tony Robbins, Jason has a knack for recognizing people's traits.

Jason now owns thirteen houses and is looking for another one to add to his portfolio. The business is turning into a family affair. His parents moved from Texas and now manage one residence for people in their fifties and sixties. On average, however, most of the residents are in their mid-thirties. Many of the houses have five or six bedrooms, with three tiers for rent: a twelve by twelve–foot guest room with a shared bath runs at $650; a guest room with a private bath is $750, and a master suite with private bath is $800. For each house, he is cash-flow positive in the range of 20 percent, or between $1,500 and $2,000 per month, above mortgage and expenses.

Jason emphasizes, though, that his business isn't about real estate, even though it has a real estate component. It's about building community and being of service to individuals who want a place to call home but aren't ready to commit to a purchase or to live alone. "Anybody can buy a house, fix it up, and rent it out," says Jason. "The going cash flow on that equation is about 3 percent. I fix it up and fill it up with quality people and cash-flow at about 20 percent."

To establish a sense of community, Jason holds an event every week. Quarterly, he throws a big party, like his Valentine's Day event, which emphasizes friendship rather than love partnerships. At these events, everyone dresses up, and activities abound, such as a cookie decorating contest.

How to Get Started

You can rent a home you own, or you can act as a host for hire and help homeowners rent their residence.

Marketing

Marketing is relatively simple for Jason. He and his two full-time handymen wear shirts when they're working. After hours, he wears another T-shirt. It's the same one he gives to residents upon the signing of their lease. That covers the soft advertising. When the need arises to fill a vacancy, Jason runs ads on about forty different websites, such as Cozy.co, Roomster.com, Zillow.com, HotPad.com, Trulia.com, and Craigslist.com—all for free.

Tips and Techniques for Building Your Business

Jason's tips and techniques for success include:

1. Start with one house. Once you've ironed out the details, then expand.

2. Define the qualities of the people you want to attract.

3. Set up house expectations—rules to live by, such as, dishes can't stay in the sink more than three hours, or no sleeping on the sofa.

4. Be a good friend. Kindness and respect are vital.

5. Expect conflict. Whenever people live together, it's not going to be all rainbows and sunshine.

6. Engage early. If there are conflicts, call them out quickly and address them.

Jason's next step: expanding into other areas of North Carolina and perhaps beyond.

Horizontal Growth

More houses and more people. Your horizontal growth plan will include maximizing the number of tenants you have and the number of properties you own.

Vertical Growth

You may be able to find people with idle homes or rooms and rent them out for a portion of the rent, often 35 percent.

Points to Remember

Know your numbers, beginning with the capitalization rate (cap rate)—the rate of return on the investment property based on the expected amount of income. You will also want to know your cash flow rate, which is the amount of cash you have left every month after paying debt and expenses (don't forget unexpected maintenance). It's easy to find these numbers; just search online for "cap rate calculator" or "cash flow rental property calculator."

Variations

Business 47: *Airbnb*

Do you have a spare room in your house that you can rent from time to time? You can charge a nightly fee for it, ranging from less than a hundred dollars a night to three times that amount. You can also add on service and cleaning fees. Prices fluctuate with the time of year, but once you become an Airbnb five-star host, you will be sought after by many.

Even if you don't own or rent your own home, you can manage an Airbnb property for others. One young couple, Mike and Mira, take on the management of other people's Airbnb spaces. This gig began when Mike offered his content writing services and Mira her photography to Airbnb hosts. Now the couple manages several locations, which takes just a few hours a day, and also receive referral fees for setting up Airbnb accounts for their clients. They find homeowners who are renting their home or room online and need help with managing the rental. These entrepreneurs do everything from remodeling the space to dropping off keys and introducing renters to the property. They serve as host, concierge, and property manager all rolled into one and can make up to 45 percent of the rent paid. Many of their clients are investors in real estate who have no intention of living in their property, just renting it on Airbnb. For more about Mike and Mira, check out their posts on Medium.com (https://medium.com/swlh/how-i-make-money-on-airbnb-without-owning-or-renting-an-apartment-c647784bdaf5).

Do you own a lama ranch, an urban farm, or a unique backyard xeriscape with local flora and fauna? You can offer hosted experiences for any number of activities to Airbnb customers. Think in terms of cooking lessons, tours around a historical area of your town, and more. Even if hosting an event isn't your thing, offer your home to someone who does have that knack.

Still another variation: there are tons of curated experiences to be found online, including directly on the Airbnb site. (See chapter 7 for more inspiration.) These experiences are growing in popularity and represent an important facet of many businesses. Technology is ubiquitous, so consumers are now seeking the best customer experience possible, whether it is in travel or services. Curate the experience to your niche clientele, and you will experience success with your business.

Business 48: *Event Accommodations*

In this niche, you focus on local events and rent only for those occasions. Think college towns, where thousands flock to big football games. A friend in Augusta, Georgia, tells me that he and all his neighbors rent their homes during the Masters Tournament. Others may rent or organize rentals in Saratoga Springs, Florida, during the thoroughbred race season or in Indianapolis during the Indy 500. The entrepreneurs I studied act as property managers, organizing online rentals on behalf of the homeowners and directing visitors to event destinations.

Business 49: *Property Manager*

The most uncomplicated approach to starting a business in this space is as a traditional property manager. Homeowners in resort towns, condo complexes, and apartment buildings are often owned by entities (corporations or homeowners' associations) or absentee owners. Rather than taking a low-paying job as a property super-intendent, start your business as a freelance property manager and manage a dozen properties! For short-term rentals, the fee is usually around 35 percent of the rental. For long-term rentals and apartments, you will receive lower fees for your service. To start this business, you need to be one part bookkeeper, one part handy-man, and one part diplomat. An even temperament will also help, because you'll be handling all the complaints. Nonetheless, it's a good business. I know many entrepreneurs as well as families that have made a multigenerational living from this service industry.

9
Life Is a Highway

Don't deliver a product; deliver an experience.
—ANONYMOUS

The future of the economy is going to look a lot like the businesses in this section, involving "Peer to peer, technology enabled goods and services available on demand within affinity networks, and other new forms of community," writes J.W. Smith in *The Independent Review: A Journal of Political Economy*. Driving is one of these enterprises.

According to the late Alan Krueger, the former chairman of President Obama's Council of Economic Advisers, the typical Uber driver is a college-educated male, married with children, and supplementing a regular job with approximately 15 hours of driving a week, consisting of 20–30 trips, and earning $300–$400 per week. The Princeton economist found that 80 percent of Uber drivers are UberX drivers and that the largest market is Los Angeles, with Miami and Austin growing quickly.

There are lots of other ways to make money driving as an entrepreneur. Let's look at a few.

Business 50: *Ride Sharing*

Working with companies like Uber and Lyft enables you to use an asset you already own (your car) to generate income. Check Uber's and Lyft's requirements in your state. If your car is not that great, explore HyreCar.com.

Business 51: *App-Based Deliveries*

If your car isn't appropriate for ride-sharing, UberEats, DoorDash, Seamless, Instacart, and GrubHub allow you to be your own boss and still make money with your vehicle.

Customers want orders fulfilled quickly. Amazon Flex is the solution to get deliveries to customers faster. You can earn $18–$25 an hour by scheduling blocks of availability on the Amazon Flex app. You pick up packages from the Amazon warehouse, and the app gives you directions to the delivery location. Amazon only hires at certain times in certain markets, so once you apply, you may have to wait for them to contact you when they are hiring in your area.

Business 52: *Rent Out Your Car*

Through services like turo.com or Getaround.com, turn your car's downtime into money. Think of it as Airbnb for your car! With Wrapify.com, you can turn your car into a rolling billboard. It is an app-based service that matches you with a campaign from companies who will fully or partially wrap your car with their message.

Business 53: *Elder and Child Transport*

On ElderCare.com, you can find engagements to transport elders in your community. You can transport children ages six and up through HopSkipDrive.com, which operates in California and Colorado.

10

Rentals

I never dreamed about success. I worked for it.
—ESTEE LAUDER

I'm starting this chapter with an example of a multimillion-dollar enterprise because I want to show you the kind of business you can grow if you work hard, help people, and make good decisions. You can start in the event planning, setup, and decorating businesses. Then you can organically achieve vertical growth by building out the equipment rental part of the business. In the beginning, you will supply your labor to plan and setup events while renting the equipment from others, but over time you will accumulate the equipment: the chairs, tables, decor, chafing dishes, stage curtains, and other items that typically support a party, event, or business conference. You will then rent them out in addition to your planning and setup services.

Business 54: *Rental World*

Rental World in South Texas is a mature, diversified general rental company with five locations and a central office and warehouse. Rental World has thousands of items to rent. They fall into two broad categories: equipment and events.

Equipment rentals range from minibulldozers and chainsaws to scaffolding and pressure washers. They have a robust sales department for used equipment too.

How to Get Started

Event rentals include wedding, party, and conference equipment. The party equipment can be very specialized. For weddings, your client may want a beautiful arbor for their beach wedding, but for their child's seventh birthday party, they will want a bounce house.

As you gradually build this part of the business, focus on a niche such as weddings or holiday themes until you build enough cash flow to add equipment in other niches. When it comes to the rental side of the business, if you were a holiday decorator, you would want to accumulate only holiday decorations at the beginning of your venture.

Tips and Techniques for Building Your Business

- Start by piggybacking on a successful operator.
- Break into the business by exploring new territories or moving into a competitor's territory. If you live in a city, see if the local operator will allow you to develop the rural areas as an independent contractor for him.
- Look to industry partners, such as the manufacturer of the toilets for support, training, and sometimes even financing of units. Polyjohn.com is a good example.

Horizontal Growth

With the different twists on rentals as shown above, you can see the many opportunities for horizontal growth, providing different products to ever increasing client segments.

Vertical Growth

I laid out a good example of vertical growth with the wedding planner and holiday decorator ideas. If you are a wedding planner, you can expand vertically into renting the equipment and decor. You can even add music, food, and lodging to the planned wedding for full vertical integration. It's the same for a holiday decorator. You begin the business with just your time and labor but expand vertically into renting the decor and equipment.

Business 55: *Portable Restrooms and Trailers*

Continuing the theme of rentals, I want to introduce you to the $15 billion business of poo. Grandview research estimates that the global portable toilet rental market will grow at a steady compound annual growth rate of 7.3 percent through 2025. For names like Port-A-Can, Porta John, Lavish Loo, and Royal Restrooms, poo equals profits. A standard portable rental toilet could cost $175–$225 per day, while the luxury restroom trailers highlighted below rent for up to $3,000 per day! The cost to buy the unit, however, is only around $700, so you make your cost of material back with only four days of rental. (A unit compliant with the American Disabilities Act may cost upward of $2,200.)

Of course, no business is that easy. The cost to transport the units and vacuum or pump the refuse is more than the cost of the toilets themselves. It can be well worth it. I've observed companies deploying a couple of hundred toilets and grossing nearly $13 million per year.

The demand is high. In addition to the need at events, nearly every construction site in America is required to have adequate restroom facilities for workers (at a minimum, every construction site will have a rented toilet and dumpster).

The first way to break into the business is to obtain a route. Go to toilet rental companies in your area and offer to develop a route or territory of customers (maybe where they are not currently represented), and place their toilets using their transport truck and pump truck. You will find the customers (contractors, event promoters), transport the toilet, and service it for the duration of the rental period. You will ask for a percentage of the rentals rather than working for a wage.

Working a route as a contractor or entrepreneur isn't a new idea. In an article in *Entrepreneur* magazine, Kimanzi Constable tells how, at age nineteen, he convinced a Sara Lee route franchisee to train him so he could cover for the operator while he was on vacation. Once the other franchisees and route operators learned about his business and services, he had a full schedule for the next two years helping others cover their routes, earning over $100,000 per year. It cost him nothing to start.

Check out these variations on the portable toilet rental business:

The Comforts of Home Services, Inc., in Aurora, Illinois (http://www.cohsi.com), produces luxury specialty trailers. Think about that fancy wedding party at the beach or outdoors: the partygoers need to visit the facilities frequently. Rather than the tiny, uncomfortable plastic porta potty, this company produces trailers with porcelain fixtures, hot and cold running water, air conditioning, and music—just like home! Fancy partygoers might wince at going into a plastic can, but will enjoy a stop at these luxury comfort stations. They rent from $950 to $3,000 per day.

I think it would be fun to take an empty trailer or trailer chassis and build fancy bathrooms in it. With a basic knowledge of plumbing, electrical, and welding, you could easily build these on weekends. Another good idea would be to convert field office trailers. During construction or exploration booms like the Permian or South Dakota oil sands rush, thousands of square, white office, bunk, and restroom trailers were deployed. Many now sit idle on lots all over the West. Why not convert some of them into fancy mobile restrooms? I've found used trailers online in the $900–$3,000 range.

Swanky Restrooms (http://www.swankytrailers.com) is a female-owned small business that provides portable sanitation in Michigan. The owner, Gretchen Menard, is terrific. Check out her "Riding Shotgun with Gretchen Menard" videos on YouTube videos, and learn about the business.

Direct Drainage (www.directdrainage.net) rents portable toilets and mobile restroom trailers but has an added business (horizontal integration): since they already have the pump trucks to clean portable restrooms, their trucks also pump out cesspools. (A cesspool is part of a typical septic tank setup).

Business 56: *Sporting Equipment*

Does your family have extra bikes, standup paddle boards, skis, and other sports items in your garage? Rent these for $15–$30 a day (less than the local guy on the beach), and you'll be on your way to some extra cash. If you own an Airbnb, you can add the rental to your featured amenities.

11

The Mobile Explosion

This concept that starting a company is so hard and that you'll never make it is a conspiracy concocted by the rich and powerful to keep you from trying—and you've fallen for it.
—JASON CALACANIS, TECHNOLOGY ENTREPRENEUR, ANGEL INVESTOR, AND THE HOST OF THE POPULAR PODCASTS "THIS WEEK IN STARTUPS" AND "ANGEL."

In this chapter, we'll explore the many options available if you have a set of wheels (motorized or human-powered), a little ingenuity, elbow grease, and perhaps some equipment. Communities, businesses, and individuals need a number of services, and if you go to them, they'll pay big bucks to be spared many inconveniences.

When starting a mobile business, you will want to start by knowing the local rules and regulations that pertain to you. These rules will mostly apply to retail and food businesses. Service businesses, such as mobile repairs, may not require the same level of permitting as resellers. You can go to https://www.municode.com/ to find your city's municipal code. You might want to contact your local economic development center for additional free assistance. You can also find a helpful YouTube video by Jeanine Romo, a mobile retail consultant for the American Mobile Retail Association, which describes how to find out which permits and licenses you need to operate as a mobile retailer.

Mobile Businesses for the Community

Business 57: *Graffiti Removal and Abatement*

Graffiti vandalism (or art, as some people see it) is on the rise worldwide. Australia estimates that property damage from graffiti exceeds $1.5 billion each year, and its government spends over $25 million per year on graffiti removal, while the city of Los Angeles spends even more, over $32 million per year, removing over 30 million square feet of graffiti. The city sends out a crew of eighty people every day to remove gang tags, which are especially prevalent in South and Central LA. Private citizens, however, are often left to clean up and restore their businesses or residences themselves.

Many of these communities may be looking for someone to do the dirty work for them. Like many of our business ideas, this enables you to make good money doing things the average person does not know how to do or doesn't want to do. You will need to do some research (some of it online) to discover the specialty cleaning solutions and tools that you will need to get started. Cleaning products with clever names like Wipe Out, Krud Kutter, Goof Off, and Spray & Walk Away claim to be effective on graffiti. You will learn about different techniques that you will need to use for different types of surfaces. Porous surfaces, such as brick and raw wood, are the most difficult and sometimes require repainting. Your business will be one that both cleans and paints.

In the beginning, you may not have the cash for high-quality tools, so you will look for affordable tools to get you started.

First, you will need a power washer and a variety of buckets and brushes for the cleaning portion, along with chemicals and solutions. Check with friends and relatives to see who has a power washer. These things typically don't get used that often, and your Uncle Fred may be more than happy to lend you his power washer for a day. You may even offer to pay Uncle Fred for the use of his washer.

If you are not able to borrow a power washer, you can rent one by the hour or by the day. Rent the power washer for only the amount of time you need it for the first day.

Do the same with buckets and brushes: hit up your friends and relatives for what you need. Be sure to obtain wire brushes as well; you will need them for the tough jobs. You will likely need regular wire, stainless steel, brass, and aluminum brushes. The softer metals will go easier on some surfaces and not leave any rust behind.

When you are painting, borrow what you can; for whatever else you need, you can acquire disposable brushes, trays, and rollers from your local discount big box store. Don't worry: you will obtain better quality tools as you achieve success over time.

One small business that has made it big in this field is Graffiti Removal Services (GRS) in Portland, Oregon, which emphasizes nontoxic, water-soluble, and biodegradable systems for removing tags and other unsightly forms of vandalism. The company's website (https://removegraffiti.net) says, "While we have trucks that can get around the metro area quickly, we have also developed anti-graffiti bikes that use pedestrian paths to access graffiti in places trucks can't. Our bikes are outfitted with our proprietary cleaning products and paint matching capabilities as well as a power washer. Everything we do is designed to maintain the visual integrity of the Rose City and surrounding areas."

Mobile Services for the Home

Business 58:
Mobile Dry Clean Pickup and Delivery

You can provide pickup and delivery of dry cleaning for busy professionals who don't have the time to do it themselves. You will work with a local dry cleaner, who will do the actual cleaning. You will charge more than you pay for the cleaning.

You will need to experiment with your pricing. Either add your profit as a percentage of what you pay the dry cleaner, or add a flat fee, such as $1 or $2 per item. Test your market to see if you can add a delivery charge as well, say $5 per trip. In the beginning, you should price yourself very competitively so you can grow a large client base. Once you do, you may be able to gradually increase your prices. Work with local dry cleaners to obtain the best cleaning for the best price. You are bringing them a ton of business, so you should get a good price. Let's say the dry cleaner charges customers $6 to launder and press a pair of slacks. If you can convince them to price it at $3 to you as a bulk customer, you can charge your clients exactly the same price they can get by dropping off the items themselves. To whom would you like to pay $6 to clean a pair of pants? The place where you have to take time out of your busy schedule to drop off dirty clothes, or the guy who picks it up at your home or office and delivers it back again? This is a no-brainer!

If you have some success, you may want to rent a small location—either a stand-alone storefront, or inside a symbiotic business, such as a boutique or local clothing store. You may be able to convince the clothier to allow you to set up your pickup and delivery counter for free or at a very low rent, because it will be a value-added service to their retail customers. Remember to look for win-win situations like this.

Business 59: *Personal Chef*

If you have a talent for cooking, you can find busy working families who would love a solution that provides a convenient restaurant quality meal at home. You may also find that cooking for and catering events is also a very viable business. I know many entrepreneurs who have closed their restaurants to focus on catering, which has a much higher profit margin.

As a variation, you may want to specialize in a particular culinary niche, like vegan or gluten-free meals, to attract an even more motivated clientele.

When you are starting out, you don't need to prepare every dish yourself, especially if you can't keep up with demand. For example, when catering an event, you may find a great bakery that will prepare your breads and desserts while you focus on entrées and appetizers. You can buy and bring these fresh, quality food items to your catered event or chef-prepared meal and serve them to your happy consumer. It's not important that you personally prepare each item.

With tastes ranging from paleo to vegan and everything in between, many people don't have the time or inclination to cook good, healthy meals. Or they're tired of cooking every meal. Your culinary talents could be the answer to someone's prayers.

Here are a few more mobile services for the home to consider:

- Power washing and painting
- Screen repair
- Hot tub repair
- Porcelain repair
- Pool cleaning and servicing
- Stove vent cleaning
- Dryer vent cleaning
- Diaper service
- Locksmith (for home or business)

Mobile Businesses for the Car, Boat, and RV

Business 60: *Mobile Car Wash*

With a little investment into a van with the ability to connect to water or electricity at a residence or business building, you could be making the rounds in your community, sprucing up the exterior and interior of your customers' vehicles—or even a fleet of vehicles.

Business 61:
Mobile Mechanic for Car, Boat, or RV

Sierra Mobile RV offers mobile services to recreational vehicle (RV) owners in and around the South Padre Island area. Technicians visit customers on site to diagnose and repair any problem. Their services extend into appliance repair and replacement, leaks, roof replacement, floor repair and replacement, and other areas.

Mobile Businesses for the Office

Business 62:
Mobile Document Shred and Archive

From shredding to digital archiving, there is a lot of horizontal growth potential here. There are still mountains of papers out there that need to be digitized and shredded. The need is huge!

You can begin your business by just offering shredding, a low-tech entry. You will be surprised how many types of customers want someone to shred paper for them. As you grow, you will upgrade your shredding equipment to handle higher volumes. In the beginning, it will just be a matter of your time and hard work. A successful shredding service will pick up the customer's papers in a secure bin or bag that has a lock on it to ensure privacy. Keep the documents secure until they are shredded.

You can expand into scanning and archiving with a low-security archiving service. Then you can grow into more secure, encrypted document handling, with remote backup for highly regulated entities or businesses with sensitive nonpublic information.

Business 63: *Mobile Bookkeeper*

Demand is insanely high for people to visit small businesses once a week or once a month to catch up the books or complete tasks such as payroll, quarterly or annual payroll tax reporting, and sales tax remittances. "Can you just come over here and fix it?" is what I've heard a hundred times from clients. Folks just want help—someone to save them from the chaos.

You will be performing the work in the client's bookkeeping software and on their computer or cloud service, with little to no investment other than your time. You can grow by establishing a remote business, whereby you host the QuickBooks accountant edition along with the company file (be sure you have a bullet-proof backup). You can provide the client with financials or with a backup file they can simply load into their version of QuickBooks. This business is superscalable and can morph into a combination of mobile work and work from home. It's flexible and has very low barriers to entry.

This opportunity is differentiated from that of virtual book-keeper because in this case, you will visit the business and render aid in person instead of operating solely in the cloud.

Business 64: Mobile Geek:
Computer, Network, and Phone Repair

I must have visited a hundred geek shops in my lifetime. You know what I mean—the guy or gal in your community that repairs computers. It's often a hole-in-the-wall or garage, and there are endless benches of CPUs, laptops, cords, and monitors in a giant web of chaos. These services are essential, but have been inconsistent. Although you can use the services at BestBuy or your local repair shop, in today's fast-paced society, people want the service to come to them. Would you rather drag your computer to someone's garage or have the technician come to you? A friend of mine ran a successful mobile computer and network setup and repair business for many years under a great name: the Computer Doctor.

Another possibility is mobile phone repair. Just follow the same business model as for the computer and network services. Perhaps you could start a business offering screen replacements for phones. Working in the business community, you would visit the owner of the busted phone at their office and repair the screen on the spot.

Business 65: *Mobile or Virtual Assistant*

What does a mobile personal assistant do? Everything! Busy and successful people need someone reliable, a gal or guy Friday who can help them accomplish the myriad tasks and events that are thrown at them every day. A truly reliable person is worth their weight in gold. Of course, you shouldn't do anything that makes you uncomfortable or that demeans you. One only need watch an episode of *Real Housewives of Beverly Hills* to see bizarre and abusive relationships with personal assistants. Make it a point to find people you enjoy working with. Take a pass on the little dictators.

A mobile assistant is differentiated from a virtual assistant simply by the fact that you will visit and do more tangible tasks. A virtual assistant does virtual or digital work and operates solely in the cloud.

As a mobile assistant, try not to become an employee of any one person or entity, but freelance for several people or entities. This way, you will get more done, have higher client satisfaction, and a more profitable business model. A virtual assistant can service up to a dozen clients. In the mobile assistant space, you may find that four to six clients are more manageable.

Business 66: *Official Greeter*

Be the official greeter of new neighbors by pulling the records of new move-ins in your area from county records or other sources, such as leasing agents. Many people will need some of these services. If they move from out of the area, they will need to change to a local insurance agent or need new daycare or a new dry cleaner.

Visit each home with a welcome bag, basket, or box. Your "welcome kit" will include helpful information about the neighborhood as well as a list of preferred service providers, such as dry cleaners, dog sitters, handymen, plumbers, insurance agents, accountants, financial advisors—almost any neighborhood business.

You will be soliciting sponsorship from the preferred service providers. In essence, they will be paying you through a monthly membership subscription to make these visits. Be sure to keep track of your visits, including all names, addresses, phone numbers, and email addresses of the new neighbor.

Tips and Techniques for Building Your Business

- Use social media to promote your business. Be sure to create a business page on Facebook, LinkedIn, and Google.
- Once you build some momentum, put up a website. It doesn't necessarily bring you traffic but validates your business to clients who are checking you out.
- Think of a memorable name for your business like Mobile-Meals, MobileChew, Mobile Party (party setup), ReadyAssist, Helpifi, or MobileStroll (dog walking). Express your unique value proposition!

Horizontal Growth

Horizontal growth possibilities abound in this group of mobile businesses. The key is finding more clients and/or selling more products and services to your existing clients. For example, if you do mobile cell phone repairs, you can provide cell phone accessories to your clients, such as protective cases and screen savers. To expand your client base, you can build centers of influence in business communities. If you have established a good circle of clients at the General Motors office complex, you can create a similar center of influence at the Ford complex or the United Auto Workers (UAW) headquarters. They are compatible constituencies, but in different locations. Provide a low-cost or free repair to an influential person in your target community, continue to do a good job, and watch the referrals flow in, doubling your customer base.

Vertical Growth

If you are a mobile food business, you can achieve vertical growth by moving up the distribution supply chain, perhaps by growing your own vegetables and positioning yourself as all-natural. If you are in the computer repair business, you may expand vertically into building and selling computers. Offer extended on-site repair warranties to motivate customers to buy your custom machines.

12

Culinary Delights

I think careful cooking is love, don't you?
The loveliest thing you can cook for someone who's close to you
is about as nice as a valentine you can give.

—JULIA CHILD

Food is the heart and soul of families, cultures, and many life events and business functions. It's often the center of conversation as we gather with friends and family and share our delight. Additionally, many people turn to cooking for a relaxing activity at the end of a day or the focus of a yearly vacation.

In this section, you'll be inspired to tap into your culinary curiosities and perhaps find a way to add a sizable chunk to your income.

Business 67: *Culinary Experience Educator*

German baking is a lifelong love for Sabine Friedrich-Walter, the San Diego resident who was born in Hamburg, Germany, and lived there for much of her adult life. However, her culinary expertise hasn't always been a means to make a living for this mother of two and grandmother of one—until recently.

A few years ago, Friedrich-Walter had a conversation with some acquaintances, who also hailed from Germany, about their inability to find good German breads and pastries in their local stores. It dawned on her to begin baking bread and selling her creations to the same people who lamented the lack of native culinary treats.

"Yet I ran into a problem," explains Friedrich-Walter, who moved to the US in 2000. "Because I insist on using high-quality ingredients, the cost of baking the bread increased prices so much that no one wanted to buy my bread."

Not to be daunted, Friedrich-Walter's next step was to offer baking classes in private homes. That worked for a time until the hostesses balked at sharing their space with strangers.

Nonetheless, word of mouth had created an ever-growing following for Friedrich-Walter. Again, ingenuity and perseverance was called for. She approached City Farmers Nursery, touted as "San Diego's source for organically maintained plants, organic soils, and homesteading supplies." In addition to selling plants and gardening supplies, there's a cafe and education space. Her willingness to make a request paid off. She now offers her signature "Sourdough from Scratch" course. Participants learn to use wild yeast, sourdough, and other starter cultures for bread baking. While the bread isn't baked on premises, participants take their starter home, complete with feeding instructions.

At the time of this writing, Friedrich-Walter, who owned a store in Hamburg that she describes as a mix between Crate & Barrel and World Market, is looking to partner with other venues to increase her offerings, including apple strudel. She also wants to continue sharing her philosophy of healthy eating, seeded from her European roots. She's also considering creating online video courses to share her love of German baking far and wide.

These types of business often explode because of word of mouth referrals. Having a Facebook page with hours of operation, the types of services, and a little bit about your story is also helpful. Posting to Instagram and Twitter help as well.

Becoming more involved in the community and joining the Chamber of Commerce; attending meet-ups—or even hosting your own—will add to your visibility. Many communities also have Nextdoor, where, much like Facebook, you can connect with your community and share the news that you are open for business.

Tips and Techniques to Build Your Business

1. Do something you love.
2. Keep your standards high. Never skimp on quality.
3. Be flexible and rise above your obstacles.

Horizontal Growth

Teach more classes to more people in more places. This may include teaching in different partner locations, rented locations, or even online! Wouldn't it be great to teach from home, on camera, and have paid subscribers from all over the world?

Vertical Growth

Become a host or hostess for other teachers with other specialties. Many Airbnb hosts open their homes to local celebrity chefs, such as Nonna's Handmade Pasta with Grandma (see business 45).

Variations

Business 68: *Raw Foods*

Teach people how to incorporate raw foods in their diet, as Joletta Cason did. Her services are coaching, cooking courses, grocery store tutorials, pantry and refrigerator Makeovers, healthy habit education, and speaking. Yours might include, for example, an alternative and holistic health service. You can learn more about her venture on her Facebook page: https://www.facebook.com/ rawandrealkitchenwithjoletta/.

13

Virtual Teaching

You can't give what you don't have. Make time each morning,
before the sun rises, to fuel your mind and fill your heart.
Empty people don't make inspirational heroes.
—ROBIN SHARMA,
AUTHOR OF *THE MONK WHO SOLD HIS FERRARI*

With the onset of the Internet, coupled with YouTube, Vimeo, Zoom, and other video platforms, you can teach anything you are skilled at. Whether you're a whiz at building websites or fly rods, creating crafts for the home such as seasonal wreaths, or operating specialized equipment, there are people who need your guidance.

Business 69: *Sew with Joe*

Florida's Joe Chisum is a master at teaching how to maximize the use of a computerized sewing machine. Read on to find out how he built a following so quickly that he's cutting back hours at his day job as a sewing machine repairperson.

His website, Sew with Joe (www.sewwithjoe.com), began because he had some talent in teaching people to sew with their specialized sewing machines. Purchasers of these machines were also telling him to take it further—to create a website and go on Facebook. And sew he did.

Even though he had a day job with Flash Sew & Quilt, Joe decided to take his talents to the next level in April of 2018.

"Before I had worked at this store," says Joe, "customers from previous stores would tell me that I have a good way of teaching. Some of them were retired teachers. 'You should post videos on YouTube.' I put it in the back of my mind and didn't take it anywhere until my new boss thought it was a great idea. He encouraged me to grow my own business."

Prior to his debut as Sew with Joe, he had been working for small sewing stores for a dozen or so years, repairing and selling sewing machines, plus teaching customers how to use the new generation of computerized sewing machines.

For a little while, Joe was hot and cold about the idea. "I made a couple of videos and posted them to the company Facebook page," he explains. "They were well received and got a lot of attention"—so much so that someone who does something similar was bent out of shape by Joe's competition. Fearful of stepping on anyone's toes, Joe stopped making videos.

But he didn't stay in the background for long. "In April 2019, I decided to do it the right way. I purchased a Baby Lock Solarus, which is a specific machine for sewing and embroidering. The machine retails for $20,000, and I bought it on credit at a reduced price," he said. "I started thinking that even though I was getting negative attention, it was a compliment to me. If these videos were good enough to draw the attention of someone who felt threatened, then I was on to something."

He then went on to register his company's LLC and opened up the Sew with Joe Facebook group.

"When I had everything set up for my business, the floodgates opened up. I had sixty people following on Facebook within the first week, and then, within the first month, a thousand. People from all over the world, including Australia and the United Kingdom, were visiting my page."

The viewers are home sewers thirsty for more information on how to use their machines. Joe does live videos every week on his Facebook group. Word spread within the viewers' communities, and soon there were over 5,000 members.

Joe also posts videos are also posted to his employer's Facebook group, Flash Sew and Quilt in Naples and Fort Myers, Florida. "I do videos on features and menus. The machine is heavily computerized, and I focus more on modern embroidery," says Joe. "I talk slow and give people a chance to follow along. The viewers can easily understand what I'm teaching. I've grown in popularity fast."

Making Money

At first, Joe didn't go into his business with an elaborate business plan—or with the intention of making money. "My plan at first was to grow in popularity. I created a community on Facebook that learns together," he explains. "But I had a limit on what I would do for free. When I attracted a regular following and had my name out there for a couple of months, in June of 2019, I decided to sell extra projects viewers could buy for a nominal price."

Joe creates a video of the specialized embroidery project and sells it for $10 or $20. At the time he began selling his projects, there were about 2,000 members, and the purchase rate was about 5 percent, then it became 10 percent.

"In the month of June, I had three projects to purchase. Then in the month of July, I offered a membership program for $20 a month," he says. "Viewers knew the value based on the month I had done before. I had a few subscribers the first month, about 200 subscribers, and from there it grew by word of mouth." In May 2020, he had over 9,400 subscribers.

Chisum had little mentoring on building a business—he just went with his gut. "I don't think I knew what I was doing with my business strategy," he explains. "I came up with an idea and a plan month by month, and it worked."

Next steps? "Since I work six days a week at the store, and I don't get as much yield as I do in my business, it's time to cut back on my hours and spend more time growing Sew with Joe," he adds. You can find out more about Sew with Joe at: https://www.facebook.com/groups/sewwithjoe/.

How to Get Started

Joe's business model illustrates one of the most powerful themes for entrepreneurs—find your niche and build on it. Throughout this book, you are reading stories about people who have found a niche in which they have talent, experience, or passion. They build their business in this niche, this area of specialization, or focus on a client segment. This is effective because specialization in a niche area creates a more satisfying and consistent client experience. (My coffee experience is usually more consistent and satisfying at Starbucks than at the local diner.) In the teaching, coaching, and subscription businesses, specialization creates a curated experience for your customer, which often includes a community of other like-minded consumers, with whom you share this unique learning journey.

Unique is beautiful. I want you to understand how unique you are as a human being. You are wonderfully made in God's image, yet you are completely unique compared to every other person. There are nearly 8 billion people on the planet, but there is only one you. Whatever business you choose, make it 100 percent yours. Carve out your niche, and let it be your differentiator. Joe's niche is computerized sewing machines, yet it is Joe himself, and his patience and style, that make his business totally and uniquely his. Be a good person, and let that shine in your work and in your business.

Let's take a quick look at the evolution of Joe's business model. First, he created interesting videos related to his work and shared them for free while building a community around their shared interest. Then he began selling videos one at a time for $10 and then $20 each to 5 percent of his 2,000 followers. If he sold one video a month to the 5 percent, then his earnings were $1,000 per month, which he says grew to $2,000, and then $4,000 per month as his penetration rate grew from 5 percent to 10 percent, and his price rose from $10 to $20 each video.

A few months later, Joe took a big risk and shifted from his reliable unit sales model to a subscription model, charging $20 per month to what is now 600 subscribers (at the time of our interview). If you multiply $20 x 600 subscribers, you have a monthly gross revenue of $12,000, which equates to $144,000 per year of gross income.

There is a powerful lesson here for those of you who are currently in or considering a business in the teaching, lessons, and coaching industry. Most entrepreneurs I know have built their business on a model of charging per lesson or per hour. But look at the cash flow potential of the subscription model. It provides the entrepreneur with consistent recurring revenue, although it also requires that the teacher deliver consistent value to the subscribers.

You will read stories about other entrepreneurs in this book who are teaching and coaching in different areas of interest, and I want you to keep the subscription revenue model in mind as you consider them. Even if the entrepreneur I feature does not use a subscription fee, you may combine these two ideas. How about cooking lessons or a writing coaching business built on a subscription model?

Marketing

The marketing plan for this business is mostly digital but will include creating flyers for existing and prospective buyers of sewing machines, or whatever niche you're offering lessons in. The flyers will point prospective clients toward your digital presence on Facebook or your website. If you create a website, you will want to optimize it for the most common searches people make when looking for information on their hobby or product.

Think about the words you might use in searching for someone like you, and use those words or phrases in your copy. In Joe's situation, the phrases and words would include the manufacturer and model of the sewing machine, as well as "how to," or other phrases unique to the activity, such as embroidery or stitch pattern.

Of course, like many startups, social media is your best venue not only to reach prospective customers but to create a community around an interest, hobby, or product. Joe chose Facebook because a page is easy to create there.

You will note that Sew with Joe is a private group rather than a traditional business page. On his SewwithJoe.com page, he offers the subscriptions for $20 monthly. You will also note that he has specific deliverables that come with a subscription. You will want to do the same. Be sure they are specific and well defined. People want to know what they are receiving for their monthly fee. Joe offers instructional videos, PES files (computer-aided manufacturing files containing embroidery instructions for a sewing machine to stitch a pattern onto a piece of fabric), digitizing instructions, stitching instructions, and example pictures.

Building a community around your niche is crucial. Some entrepreneurs like Sloane Davis, who operates Pancakes & Push-ups, a fitness lifestyle site, build community solidarity. She calls her subscribers the "Sloane Squad." Terri Turner's cooking site, No Crumbs Left, calls her subscribers "Crumbles." How will you create your community's identity?

Tips and Techniques for Building Your Business

Joe suggests: "Find a niche and master it. The sewing machine industry is so specific. I first became successful as an employee because I was a sewing machine repairman at a time when there were few knowledgeable repairpersons. The confidence that grew from that made me better."

If you're an employee, "be loyal to yourself first. And look for collaborative opportunities. There's a relationship between myself and my store. While I included tips for previous models, I show my followers what they can do on the top-of-the-line machine and show features that only the new one can do. It's subtle, but it has led to more purchases for the store, and the store in turn promotes me through their advertisements.

"All your second guessing is going to hold you back. Don't second-guess yourself. You can take yourself much further than you believe you can."

Variations

Lynda Weinman taught herself graphic design on a Mac by reading the instruction manual. Eventually, she taught graphic design at the local college and acquired the domain Lynda.com so she could offer videos to her students. Over time, Lynda.com morphed into an online learning library, with a subscription model that never charged more than $25 monthly. In 2015 Lynda.com was acquired by LinkedIn for $1.5 billion and is now LinkedIn Learning.

Horizontal Growth

Many entrepreneurs in the teaching space write books on their niche. This will help you diversify. Lynda.com purchased a website similar to itself in Europe containing a learning library in Dutch, French, and German.

Vertical Growth

There is limited vertical growth in this space. The distribution channel is through the ISP (Internet service provider or social media platform), most of which are huge. Successful entrepreneurs like Joe and Lynda focus on insane levels of horizontal growth.

How to Get Started

Share the word of your expertise, not only with your friends and family, but on these sites as well:

- For language and music instruction, visit Lessonface: www .lessonface.com.
- For multiple subjects, Varsity Tutors is the place to search: www.varsitytutors.com.

- If you're accomplished in English, check out VIP Kid (www .vipkid.com/teach) and GOGOKID (teacher.gogokid.com).

Tips and Techniques for Building Your Business

Lisa suggests:

1. Do something you *love*! There is no point in starting a business if you don't fully love and support your own path and passion.

2. Be patient. You may not see an immediate success, and you will see some downfalls. Make some tweaks, brainstorm for other elements to add, but stay true to your idea.

3. Don't let people take advantage of you or lower your standards— or your rate. You are worth every penny, and people will pay.

Business 70: *Online Tutor for Standardized Tests*

Again, here you can communicate with clients through email and do your tutoring using video conferencing tools from the likes of Skype, Slack, GoToMeeting, or Zoom. Certification is not required to be a SAT tutor, but it may look good on your website. You can take a three-hour training from Harvard College and obtain a SAT tutor certificate (https://publicservice.fas.harvard .edu/sat-tutor-certificate). In addition, you may want to score in the ninetieth percentile on SAT practice to sharpen your proficiency. There are numerous practice versions online.

Business 71: *College Entrance Consultant*

Provide understanding of college admissions, test prep, essay requirements, personal statements, and financial aid to families, who will pay handsomely for competent assistance in helping their children gain admission to the school of their dreams.

Essentially, anything that you teach face-to-face can be taught virtually. All it takes is a little time, a Zoom, Vimeo, or YouTube account, your computer camera or a smartphone, and you're in business.

Having a bachelor's or graduate degree in education or education counseling is helpful but not required. You may also consider joining the Higher Education Consultants Association (HECA) if you have a bachelor's degree and meet their other criteria.

14

Virtual Reality

The most common form of despair is not being who you are.
—SØREN KIERKEGAARD

In today's gig society, with Internet access readily available around the world, many people are able to work from home while fly-fishing in the mountains of Montana, lounging on the beaches of Belize, or hiking the hills of the Alps. All you need is a good laptop, Internet access, a Zoom or Skype account, and any other software that will allow you to share your skills and talents with those who lack the time or talent to get the job done.

Whether you're a whiz at numbers, a wordsmith extraordinaire, or a master at moving projects or teams, there's no reason for you to be tied to one location if your dream is to have your office wherever you want and to work when you want.

In this part, you'll find just what you need to kickstart your virtual business in the cloud.

Business 72: *Writing Coach*

When Kathy Sparrow was in high school, she was told she would never be a writer. For a time, she believed the incomprehensible and irresponsible mandate that her guidance counselor placed upon her future. For about a decade, she followed his script, studying business and accounting in high school and community college. However, when she was in her mid-twenties, her soul could not be quieted any longer.

At the time, Kathy was a mom to two young children, married to an unkind man, and working part-time as liaison for a US congressman in New York state. On Tuesday evenings, she would carry home the government-issued typewriter, and on Wednesdays (her only day off during the week) she would write while her children were in school. She soon began writing profiles for a local community arts paper, meeting artists, writers, dancers, and musicians who made the community just two hours from New York City their weekend homes.

As time progressed and Kathy's portfolio increased, she began writing for other publications and soon began offering editorial services as well. Her first big break as an editor came when she was living in Indianapolis and was hired as a part-time proofreader for the publisher of the For Dummies book series.

A decade or so into her writing career, Kathy noticed that when people asked her what she did for a living and her response was, "I am a writer," they often remarked, "I always wanted to be a writer. I just don't know how to start."

In addition to writing and editing, Kathy began teaching others to write. Initially, she would meet individuals in coffee shops for one-on-one coaching. Over time, as the Internet grew and services such as Skype and Zoom became available, she began meeting her clients virtually.

Kathy found success in her field without any formal training as a writer. She simply loved to read and write, and her natural talents have taken her far. Initially she didn't possess a college degree, but after realizing her love of teaching, she returned to the classroom in her forties and now has a master's degree in English. She continues to teach private clients and also teaches marketing for authors online at the university level, as well as composition and technical writing classes at a community college and a private university.

Kathy's grit and love of writing took her from being someone who always longed to write to having several channels of income from her writing skills. She not only writes her own blogs, books, and courses, she proofreads, edits, and ghostwrites all types of materials, from letters, résumés, bios for websites, marketing materials, and more. At this writing, she's launching a new program to guide families in preserving their legacy stories to make sure that precious memories are available for future generations.

To find out more about Kathy's services, visit kathysparrow.com.

How to Get Started

According to Kathy, the hardest part of writing is the beginning: sitting down at a blank screen and hoping the words will flow. She likens writing to working out and advises a fifteen-minute practice each day. From there, your writing skills will grow. Reading is also important. "The more we read, the better we write," she shares.

Once your skills are honed, you can begin offering your services to others. Many people hate writing, so the market is extensive. Many of Kathy's clients are well-established businesspeople who have little time for writing but have many ideas they want to share with the world.

Marketing

Word of mouth keeps Kathy busy. She's built her business on doing what she is called to do. However, she keeps herself visible by having a website, a LinkedIn profile, and several social media channels—Facebook, Twitter, and Instagram. There she shares not only tidbits about her own life but tips on writing and client profiles as well.

For more assertive marketing, LinkedIn has a ProFinder service. Here people on LinkedIn put out a request for proposals. The proposal is a simple statement explaining why you're fit for the job; if the person or company is interested, they will reach out to you. For more details, see www.linkedin.com/profinder.

There are also a number of sites where you can list your talents and services, such as Upwork (www.upwork.com) or Freelancer (www.freelancer.com/info/how-it-works).

Tips and Techniques for Building Your Business

Kathy's advice is:

1. Be the best writer you can be. It's a journey. We're never perfect. It's a path of mastery.

2. Build your portfolio, even if it means writing $50 profiles in the beginning. Soon you'll be able to charge between $55 and $125 an hour wordsmithing. In the beginning, after I left my day job, I was doing virtual assistant work for other entrepreneurs.

3. Be visible. Build your own buzz by making sure people know how to find you.

Variations

Business 73: *Virtual Editor*

Every writer needs a good editor to read the content for clarity and to make sure the punctuation is correct, words aren't dropped from phrases or sentences, and spelling is spot-on. You can do this in a virtual environment, exchanging drafts on Trello.com or Google Docs.com. You can use the same startup procedure, marketing, and tips and techniques as for the writing coach business.

Business 74: *Blogger*

We've already looked at some possibilities for blogging in business 5. Blogging can give you an outlet for your ideas, passions, and words of wisdom while attracting sponsors and advertisers by building an audience. You can go to Wordpress.org or a similar service and start your blog page in mere moments. Build an audience, and then sell sponsorships.

There also are places where you can guest blog. Get paid $75 to $100 per blog of 900–1500 words on sites like Freelance Mom: The Source for Professional Moms. Check out their guidelines at www .freelancemom.com/guest-post-guidelines/

Find other places to blog by reading "Top Nine Places to Find Paid Blogging Jobs" on The Balance Small Business: www.the balancesmb.com/top-places-to-find-paid-blogging-jobs-2531559.

Business 75: *Social Media Manager*

Do you love to create memes and thoughtful, inspiring posts on social media? Small businesses usually don't have time to spend hours creating content. Here you can make between $25 and $30 per hour helping to market other businesses. Social media managers help other businesses run their social media game. This usually entails helping them set up their pages and accounts properly and then posting on their behalf.

Business 76: *Virtual Bookkeeper*

Maybe writing isn't up your alley, but you're a whiz at numbers. We've already looked at some possibilities for mobile bookkeepers in business 63. Virtual bookkeepers can provide bookkeeping, accounting, and tax services that customers, especially business owners value. Great bookkeepers are hard to find and keep say many business owners. If they can find someone reliable for a fraction of the cost of a full-time employee, they will hire you and keep you busy forever. You can bridge the proximity gap and data sharing by using an online accounting program like QuickBooks/cloud or one of the others I mention in the services and tools section at the end of the book.

In an article in ThePennyHoarder.com, Ben Robinson, a certified public accountant and business owner who teaches others to become virtual bookkeepers, stated that many virtual bookkeepers can make up to $60 per hour.

Business 77: *Virtual Back Office*

Some customers need more than an assistant. They need a more robust solution to the administrative burdens they are currently bearing. Dynamic Advisor Solutions provides full back- and middle-office support to wealth advisors and advisory firms. They can outsource the entirety of their back office, billing, compliance, and investment administration to Dynamic, while receiving the professional services and consulting they need to grow organically and strategically.

Another example of the virtual back office is in the medical field. The process of submitting services for payment to Medicare, Medicaid, and insurance companies is complex and specialized. Many doctors' offices fall behind on claim submissions and fail to collect reimbursements for services rendered because they lack the expertise or manpower to properly code and submit for these reimbursements. If you've worked as a Medicare, Medicaid, or insurance coder or utilization review person at a doctor's office or hospital, you can freelance to these outsource companies while working from home. You can also create your own company to do coding and submissions for your local doctors' offices. Most docs spend far too much in payroll expense for full-timers in these positions and still run way behind on billing and reimbursements. It is the Achilles' heel of the local medical practice. You can help.

Variations

Business 78: *Virtual Assistant*

Are you an organized, detailed-oriented person? Then assisting a small business owner or even a busy CEO may be the answer to your work-at-home prayers. These opportunities are often listed on Upwork, ZipRecruiter, and Facebook. There's also a Virtual Assistant Network Association. Visit its site: VAnetworking.com. According to this organization, you can earn between $25 and $100 an hour, depending on the services you offer.

Business 79: *Personal Assistant*

Some people are willing to pay you just to do their stuff—even if they're not in business! Think of the folks in *Real Housewives of Beverly Hills*.

Business 80: *Personal Shopper*

Do you love shopping? Or picking out clothes? Shop for someone else and get paid to do it. During the pandemic, Instacart was hopping by providing grocery shopping services for those who were not willing to don a mask and head to the store. Many are realizing this might just be the way to go from now on.

Business 81: *Project Manager*

Sometimes people want someone who can handle a myriad of tasks and jobs—a get-it-done kind of person. Virtual task and project management is in demand.

Marketing Your Virtual Services

This is easily done on your social media pages, such as Twitter, Facebook, and LinkedIn. Don't forget Instagram and YouTube. Images and videos are some of the most powerful communication tools available. Create a meme or image for Instagram with a sample of your work. Place a link to your website in your Instagram profile. For YouTube, make a short, sincere video telling people about what you love about your business. You will want to post your services for bid on freelance marketplaces like Fivver and UpWork. You will find more on these marketplaces in chapter 20, "Selling Your Services."

15

Build Their Buzz

I strongly believe that missionaries make better products.
They care more. For a missionary, it's not just about the business.
There has to be a business, and the business has to make sense,
but that's not why you do it. You do it because you have
something that motivates you.

—JEFF BEZOS

If you talk to most business owners, the task they dislike the most and have the least amount of time for is marketing. Yet continual marketing is necessary to ensure long-term success. One way to market a business is through promotional products, such as pens, coffee mugs, sweatshirts, and hats. Just think: when was the last time you stepped out of your house and did *not* see someone sporting a T-shirt, jacket, or hat with the name of a sports team, a destination, or a business? In this chapter, I'm going to share the success story of Bling by Beverly. Read on for more inspiration.

Business 82: *Bling by Beverly*

In 2008, Beverly was a teacher and a mom with teenagers who were active in school sports and band. She was very involved in the booster club and eventually ended up being the go-to mom for spiritwear, such as team or band T-shirts. These usually had traditional silkscreened or embroidered images of the team logo or mascot. At some point she had a shirt made for herself with the kid's bulldog mascot with an overlay of sequins or rhinestones. The other booster club moms raved about it and wanted one for themselves. Once other clubs, schools, and teams saw the shirts, they wanted one too.

So Beverly quickly went from supplying her own booster club with shirts to supplying all the local booster clubs, teams, and bands in the area with blingwear.

She attended a trade show and purchased a small booth, displaying a few samples of the blinged-out shirts. The response, demand, and subsequent orders were overwhelming. At first, she would simply design the shirts, order them from suppliers who had the machines and staff to produce the shirts, and resell them at a markup.

At first, her sales were only wholesale. A club or team would order a dozen or twenty identical shirts, so the ordering was simple. Eventually Beverly discovered that many people wanted the shirts customized with their names, usually on the back. Beverly pivoted to providing personalized shirts, and now even offers completely customized shirts. The newest embroidery machines can stitch up to four rows of sequins or rhinestones at a time from an image uploaded to a computer program—so the sky is the limit when it comes to images or ideas that people want on their shirts.

No Money Down!

Beverly bought the first shirt for herself. As a result, when the other moms ordered shirts, she already know how much they would cost, so she collected the money from them upfront before ordering. Subsequent orders for booster clubs and teams were also prepaid, so there was no upfront cash outlay to start this business.

Later, Beverly wanted to produce the shirts herself but didn't have the time, so she took on a partner, who did all the production while Beverly did the sales. In time, they each formed their own companies, with one doing the manufacturing and the other sales. Although this is not the path that most people take, it is an interesting arrangement. They have avoided the heartburn, power struggles, disagreements, and business divorces that often accompany partnerships. The profits are split, but each person maintains their independence, autonomy, and can grow their business any way they want without needing a partner's consensus.

How to Get Started

Bev has a secret weapon in her marketing plan. It cost nothing, works 24/7/365, and reaches 12,000 people. It is her Facebook page (@BlingbyBeverly). It is not complicated, wasn't engineered by a consulting company, and doesn't use "skin" to get likes; nonetheless, Bling by Beverly has over 12,000 followers.

One way Beverly gets followers and responses is to post at times she thinks her core audience—teachers and sports moms—is likely to see them. She posts early in the morning (because her audience is up early) and around lunch, so that after they have eaten and are having their midday Facebook cruise, they'll see her posts. Finally, she posts at 9:00 p.m., because moms are busy through their power hours—after school or work through bedtime—but after the dishes are done and the family is settled down, they can relax with their smartphone and Facebook. At that time, Beverly's blingy post should be at the top of their news feed.

Tips and Techniques to Start Your Business

- Use an established embroiderer and silkscreener in the early stages of your business, so you don't have to invest in equipment and labor or learn how to operate the equipment. You will make an agreement with them to buy in bulk at lower prices, so you can sell to your customers at a markup.
- Use social media to put product images in front of potential customers. Post at the best time of day to reach your ideal clients. Post photos of products based on season—football in the fall, Thanksgiving in November, Christmas in December, basketball in January.
- Payment processing: make sure that people can order online via Facebook, Etsy, an Amazon storefront, or some similar service. Also, sign up with a credit card processor such as Cube, which works on a smartphone or tablet, so you can take orders at trade shows and events.
- After you have had some success, you can add products such as long-sleeve shirts, hoodies, bags, and hats. You may have begun with inexpensive cotton T-shirts, but now you can expand into technical materials like Dri-FIT (a high-performance polyester material) and high-dollar name brands like Nike or Under Armour.

Vertical Growth

You will begin selling products that are produced by an established embroiderer. After you have had some success, you can expand into the manufacturing of the items you sell by:

- Purchasing embroidery machines
- Taking a manufacturing partner

- Creating a contractual relationship (rather than a partner-ship) with someone with whom you can split the duties of purchasing and manufacturing. One of you can perform sales and marketing activities while the other orders materials and creates the products.

Business 83: *Theme Wear Variations*

The businesses I described got their start with spirit wear for middle- and high-school teams and organizations. You may also find customers attracted to other themes.

Tourism themes. If you live in Las Vegas, you might sell Vegas-themed gear, like RhineDesigns: (www.etsy.com/listing/550031008/las-vegas-shoe-martini-rhinestone-t?ref=shop_home_active_84).

Outdoor themes. Nature Gift Store (natur-gifts.com) and Wild lifeWonders.com are two examples of outdoor themed stores built around an exclusively outdoor theme. There is even a company that will provide you outdoor themed templates for your Shopify account: ThemeForest.net.

Combined themes. Rogue American and Invader Coffee evolved using independent, tough-guy, veteran-supporting, warrior themes, including the Second Amendment, freedom, patriotism, and weight lifting (www.invadercoffee.com; www.rogueamericanapparel.com).

Multiple themes. Check out Teespring or Printify (teespring.com or printify.com). Create your own designs on clothing like leggings and shirts, home decor, phone cases, and accessories and sell them on your website. TeeSpring and Printify are POD (print on demand) partners that will customize the merchandise using your design and will ship directly to your customer. (See my section on drop shippers). You don't need to keep inventory or shipping materials on hand.

16

Fur, Fin, and Feather

I think having an animal in your life
makes you a better human.
—RACHAEL RAY

Our pets, whether they're furry, feathered, or scaled, often serve a
bevy of needs, including companionship and caretaking. At times,
we even treat our pets better than our human loved ones.

According to the American Pet Products Association, in 2018,
$72.56 billion was spent on our pets. Of this, $6.1 billion of this was
on services such as grooming, training, boarding, and pet sitting.
One only need look at the proliferation of pet-oriented franchises
to see that there is unmet demand. The keynote address at the 2018
Petfood Forum was "My Pets Eat Better than Me" and included data
showing that millennials are driving online purchases, with median
prices approaching $30 per pound! Our pets are living their best
lives now, and the trend appears to favor growth in the pet supplies
and services industry.

Taking care of the needs and desires of pet owners is one area
where entrepreneurs can score and score big, like Arizona's Apple-
wood Pet Resort & Spa.

Even though we're not going to spend much time on franchise opportunities in this book (mostly because they have upfront cost and don't fit our "little to no money" startup profile), these pet franchises inform our view of the industry and the types of business opportunities that are available to you. I think the proliferation of these businesses hints at the love and enjoyment that people derive from their pets and the appeal that a pet-oriented business presents.

Pet Supplies Plus has over 400 franchise locations nationwide and was recently purchased by private equity firm Sentinel Capital Partners, indicating that Sentinel believes there is still a ton of upside potential in this space. Perhaps there is an opportunity for you to start an online business providing specialty or niche pet supplies. Organic and all-natural pet supplies are trending now.

Wild Birds Unlimited has grown to more than 340 locations worldwide. If you are a bird lover, you may want to compete with them with a more affordable online store.

Aussie Pet Mobile fits our easy startup model, providing mobile pet grooming from nearly 280 franchisees in North America. This is a brilliant business model that you could readily duplicate.

Camp Bow Wow, Dogtopia, and **Central Bark** also demonstrate the viability of this business opportunity, with its a low barrier to entry. From doggy daycare to overnight boarding, grooming, training, in-home pet care, dog walking, and waste removal, the Bow Wow service does it all. You can break into this kind of service business very quickly.

Fetch! Pet Care is a service that matches pet sitters and walkers with pet owners. I think there is still a huge unmet need in this arena, and I'll spend time on it later in this chapter.

Wag 'n Wash's success is an indicator that pet washing and grooming is still a high-demand niche that you may be able to exploit in your area without needing to buy an expensive franchise.

So if you love animals, this might be the perfect place for you to build a thriving business in your own neighborhood. Indeed this is one area where choosing just one success story was difficult. With over half of American homes owning pets, there are a number of ways to increase your income in this industry.

Business 84: *Poop Duty*

Some people love their pets but hate the cleanup. Do you have a few hours on your hands every week? Then a shovel and a bucket are all you need to be a mobile poop scooper. Scoop Soldiers is one company that touts having "trained, uniformed, background checked techs that love dogs." One weekly visit for up to four dogs is $12.99. Poop 911 in Colorado Springs charges a minimum of $9.95 to clean up your backyard. I love the name possibilities! Some of my favorites are:

Poop Troops	Yard Guards on Doody
Doody Calls	Wholly Krap!
The Poop Happens	Poop Scoop & Away
Doo Care	The Grand Poobah
The Line of Dooty	The Poop and Nothing but
Doodie Free Zone	the Poop

Super Duper Pooper Scooper	Pain in the Grass
Yaba Daba Doo Doo	Poopless in Seattle
The Great Poodini	Dr. Doo-litter
We Do Doo Doo	Bid Adieu to Poo

Business 85: *Fashionista for Dogs*

Sheryl Carr fell in love with a rescue dog, Scotty, who sported a bow tie on a pet finder site. She said, "I knew I just had to have him and started making bow ties for him and his fellow foster friends! Soon enough I had so much fabric that I wanted to expand, and Scotty's Bow Ties was created!" Her company makes bow ties and bandanas, charging between $6 and $16 for the products (scottys bowties.square.site). With a sewing machine and a little fabric, you could be well on your way to creating fashion statements for pet lovers far and wide.

Business 86: *Pesky Critters*

Not all critters are loved by all. There are times when they inhabit our spaces and become quite the nuisance. Iguana Solutions, located in South Florida, removes invasive species like iguanas, ducks, and snakes. They charge either by the hour or the animal. For instance, for $60 they will remove one iguana (www.iguana-solutions.com). You've got to check out their Instagram and YouTube channels. It's great fun watching them catch iguanas, ducks, and snakes. Jessica also puts on educational talks with live animals—popular with kids. She's done a great job of building her brand through social media, taking people inside her day-to-day, and being active in her community with educational talks. This is a great example of successful grassroots marketing and business development for any business model.

Business 87: *Military Dogs*

During the research for this book, I stumbled across an article on Gen.Medium.com: "How to Make Millions Selling Dogs to the Government" by Jake Bittle: "The story of one canine entrepreneur shows that it pays to be a military middleman."

Bittle shares the story of James Lyle, who "has earned around $3.2 million over the last decade selling more than a thousand combat dogs to the US military and the Department of Homeland Security. He buys German shepherds and Belgian Malinois from European breeders overseas and spends a few months training them to detect and locate drugs, explosives, and people." The story also reports that "Lyle earns a net profit of up to $10,000 per dog."

An initial investment of $2,000 or more is needed to make this kind of profit—along with the knowledge of how to properly train a dog to be fit for military service.

Business 88: *Leafy Companions*

Not everyone has the time or patience for caring for a pet, but they might want a little life in their house or apartment. This is where putting your green thumb to work might add more green to your bank account.

"Brooklyn-based interior plant designer Lisa Muñoz started gardening as a child alongside her grandparents in her home state of Texas," we read on the website of her business, Leaf and June (www .leafandjune.com). "The name Leaf and June combines Lisa's nickname, Leaf, (she loves plants just a little) and her influential maternal grandmother's first name, June." For approximately $2,000, Leaf will enhance your space with the perfect greenery.

An offshoot of a plant design business is a plant maintenance business. Not only do you design and place the plants, but you continue to maintain them for the home or office owner. Consider a busy office building. They want their space to look good, but what banker or broker has the time to maintain the office plants? Who else is going to do it? Enter the plant doctor! You will design and place the plants, feed and water, and replace as necessary. An even better business model is subscription or leasing the plants. You place the plants and rotate as necessary. The home or office owners pays a monthly fee and enjoys worry-free greenery while you have created a recurring income stream. It's a win-win business engagement.

How to Get Started

In addition to good old-fashioned advertising, like posting flyers on local bulletin boards and magnetic car signs, you can list your pet sitting services on PetSitter.com. Entrepreneurs can get themselves listed on this site. It's as simple as creating an account and adding your photo and other relevant information to your profile. "PetSitter.com connects your furry family members with a massive community of pet lovers, offering pet sitting, dog walking, grooming & boarding services. Whether you have a dog, cat, fish or something more exotic we can help you find someone to help care for them when you can't. Dog walkers, cat sitters, kennels, doggy daycares, pet grooming, dog sitters—you name it we've got it" (petsitter.com).

Rover.com is another place to search for jobs and post your availability. Many locations also have their own local pet-sitting service listings. Just Google "pet sitters" in your area to find others.

Otherwise, follow Jessica's example at Iguana Solutions. It doesn't matter if your business is dog grooming, plant care, or invasive species—you've got to engage in the type of guerilla marketing that you see at Iguana Solutions. She is blitzing her community digitally with Instagram, Facebook, and YouTube, but also interacts in person, with solid community engagement through her educational talks. Whom are you going to call when you have an iguana problem? Of course, the lady who did the iguana presentation at your kid's kindergarten class. Notice too that her engagement is not tasteless in-your-face solicitation; it's sharing her experiences in a sincere way and providing tons of free education both in her talks, on the website, and in the social media. Emulate this approach, and you'll succeed.

Tips and Techniques for Building Your Business

1. Start small, and look for opportunities to expand. As an example, you can start a poop scoop business in about five minutes, but it may not be enough for you to make a living, so you need to grow it by adding more customers and helpers, or secondarily by expanding into other aspects of pet care, such as dog walking, sitting, and daycare. Remember to just get started. You can take that first job tomorrow.

2. Gather testimonials of satisfied customers to add to your marketing platforms.

3. Study the businesses operating in your area, and look to fill a niche where there isn't as much competition. If there are dozens of poop scoopers, maybe look to the pet sitter niche instead. An underserved niche is often your best choice.

Horizontal Growth

Let's divide pet care into products and services. You will either sell pet products or sell a service. Of course, as you grow, you may be selling both.

Products. If you are selling products, you will strive for horizontal growth by selling more products to more people. If you're selling pet scarves online, you may want to add other products to the lineup to appeal to more people and increase your average sale per client. You may want to try a subscription model. Pet owners may want to receive a new outfit for the pooch every month! If you're selling organic pet products, you will look for ways to continually add popular products to your lineup, therefore appealing to more people or capturing more of their wallet.

Services. There are two ways to grow: deepen and strengthen your niche, or diversify.

Let's use dog walking as an example. You may want to strengthen your niche by finding more clients and eventually adding more helpers to your business. You focus on doing a really good job at just one thing. The alternative is to diversify. Your business might begin with pet sitting. Then you may add day care and end up years down the road with a pet resort and spa!

Vertical Growth

An example of vertical growth would be a business of reselling organic pet treats and then moving on to produce those treats yourself. With pet attire, scarves, and the like, you may begin selling items you bought wholesale and evolve into producing these items yourself. Later you may begin wholesaling them to other retailers. In this way, you are capturing more of the supply and distribution chain.

Variations

Variations abound in this business space. There are so many iterations and combinations of products and services that the possibilities are almost endless. Pet walking, pet sitting, training, daycare, supplies, and boarding are so interrelated and overlapping that the transitions and permutations can be really fun. What's your vision?

Business 89: *Pet Grooming*

There are subvariations in this niche as well. You may begin as a mobile groomer, which is a quick way to build customers. Your aspiration may ultimately to have a destination grooming business, like Wag 'n Wash. As a mobile groomer, you may show up and groom the animal on the customer's premises, or you may want to work toward the business model like Aussie, where you have a van, truck, or RV equipped to do your work in the vehicle.

There are lots of possibilities here. I'll present the next five ideas in order of sophistication. One may evolve to the next, requiring additional time and resources as you move from one to another.

Business 90: *Dog Walking*

Getting started is simple. Just show up and do a good job! Your investment is your time, although you may want to add a few of your own leashes in appropriate lengths as well as a few gentle lead collars, which allow you to control animals gently without putting pressure on their neck, or you might use a harness, which gives the animal a good base to pull against you. You can begin to find customers by listing your services on Petsitter.com as well as SittingforaCause.com, WagWalking.com, Bark.com, Rover.com, Care.com, and Craigslist.

A love of animals is not enough to qualify you as a great dog walker. You may also want to become informed about dog behavior and handling different sizes and breeds of animal.

According to the American Kennel Club, you should be prepared to answer some of the following questions from potential customers:

- Where will you walk my dog?
- Do you walk multiple dogs together or one at a time?
- How long will you spend with my dog on each walk?
- Are you experienced with dogs like mine?
- How long have you been a dog walker? (If they're with a dog walking service, inquire how long they've been working for the company.)
- Are you licensed, bonded, and insured?
- Can you provide client references?
- Have you participated in any pet care training, such as pet first aid?
- What's your cancellation policy?
- What happens if you are sick and unable to come on a scheduled day?

Most communities do not require dog walkers to have licenses, but most will want a general business license. Check with your local authorities and get started!

Business 91: *Pet Sitting*

This is a great entry-level business idea, which enables you to set your own schedule and define your territory, as well as providing an avenue for expansion into other pet care business segments. SittingforaCause.com, Rover.com, Wag.com, Rover.com, Bark.com, and Pet Sitters International are places where you can list your services and connect with potential clients.

Business 92: *Pet Day Care*

This business requires you to have a place where you can care for pets while mom and dad are at work or at an event. There will be license, insurance, bonding, and regulatory requirements. The Pet Care Services Association (PCSA) is a good resource for beginning your due diligence as you build your daycare business plan. The International Boarding & Pet Services Association (IBPSA; IBPSA.com) is another great resource to use as you dig into the requirements and evaluate the possibilities.

Business 93: *Pet Boarding*

One woman I know snake-sits for friends on deployment for $100 a month. The only thing she must do is clean the cage and feed a rat or two to the guest boas. The PCSA and IBPSA will continue to be good resources as you morph from daycare to overnight boarding. While boarding reptiles doesn't take up much space, once you move to boarding cats, dogs, and horses, the space requirements go way up, and sanitation and animal health become the preeminent concern.

Business 94: *Puppy Midwife/Doggy Doula*

Here you would assist pregnant dogs and their human parents through the birthing process. This can be done in person or virtually. Many of these folks have a nursing degree or are trained as vet techs, such as those who work with Karen Copley of WhelpWise, near Denver, Colorado. Copley's company rents and/or sells uterine contraction monitors and ultrasound Dopplers to veterinarians and breeders. She and her staff, which includes a staff veterinarian, offers 24/7 monitoring services during whelping and in many cases determines the best time for C-sections or veterinarian visits.

On the other side of the pond, Nicole Bottomly is a birth doula for Guide Dogs UK (www.petguide.com/blog/dog/uk-woman-has-doggy-doula-dream-job). She began her career with just a little experience under her belt as a vet tech and later as a kennel assistant. She holds the title of Brood Bitch Supervisor.

17

Gifts for All: Baskets, Boxes, and Surprises

Gift baskets and boxes, as well as subscription boxes, are the some of the easiest businesses to start. I am lumping them all into this chapter because the execution of the idea is similar across several variations of the concept. I'll start with corporate gifts, because they attract clients all year, as opposed to holiday gifts, which are seasonal. There are stories galore to show how successful this venture could be.

Business 95: *Corporate Gifts*

Nearly 80 percent of companies surveyed by the Advertising Specialty Institute (ASI) in a recent year said they expected to spend approximately $48 each on corporate gifts. In a recent article, *Forbes* set the corporate gift market at $242 billion in 2021. A 2018 *Forbes* article by Pamela N. Danziger looked to "the 'Miss Manners' of business gifting," Laura Jennings, founder of Knack, a custom gifting company in Seattle, for her insights into gifting success, based on her company's survey of 1,000 gift recipients.

Everyone surveys companies to learn their gifting habits, but nobody bothered to ask the recipients of the gifts what they thought. "Only through understanding the attitudes, expectations, and experiences of the recipients would it be possible to maximize the experience for business gift recipients, while advancing the objectives of the companies sending all those gifts," says Jennings.

In short, you should be thinking about what people want in this scenario. The best corporate gift boxes, packages, and baskets are not going to necessarily be what you like but are aimed at what your recipients want.

"Jennings says there is an etiquette of business gifting, which her company discovered by surveying the people that really matter—the recipients," writes Danziger. Jennings' checklist for successful business gifting includes:

- Give a useful item, something practical that everyone can use.
- Surround the useful item with shareable gourmet food.
- Think quality over quantity but make it themed, for example pair a cheese board with crackers and jam or a travel backpack with jerky and trail mix or coffee tumbler with high-quality coffee beans.
- Give items made in the US Specific causes might be polarizing but Made in USA is universally favored as a top values attribute in this study.
- Spend between $50–$150, with Junior level business partners in the $50–$65 range, most clients and manager/director level associates at $75–$100 and for C-suite execs, VPs and most valued clients up to $140–$160.
- Write a personally-addressed note—a no brainer! This is without a doubt the single most powerful—and cheapest—thing you can do to create a lasting personal connection with your gift.

Here are some terrific ideas that have been successful:

Vera Stewart (www.VeryVera.com) was a local caterer in Augusta, Georgia, and began sending her cakes to *O Magazine* around 1999. After ten years, Oprah chose Vera's strawberry cake as one of her favorite things and featured it in *O Magazine* in April 2009. The cake sold online for $50 for years, until the company stopped shipping cakes. This was my go-to gift for corporate clients. According to bakecalc.com, the cost of materials to bake that cake are $4.58. Shipping is charged on top of the retail price. BoxUSA.com has insulated shipping cartons from $6 to $10. Your time and profit are approximately $45 per cake.

The Brazos Bottom Pecan Pie in a Wooden Box has been another of my favorite corporate gifts over the years. These are fun to receive. You have this great wooden box to open and discover your pie! Their deluxe gift boxes include additional treats, such as toasted sugary pecans or pralines. Voted the best mail order pie in America by Bloomberg, this is an inspiration for you as an entrepreneur. Make your idea this good!

Wine Country Gift Baskets is a leader in this space. As you look through their offerings, you will notice that they have numerous baskets, tins, and boxes that have no wine at all. They have chocolate-, coffee-, and tea-themed baskets as well. Owler.com estimates that Wine Country Gift Baskets rakes in $46.5 million per year. According to giftbaskethelp.com, the markup on gift basket materials is approximately three times. So a basket that has $10 in materials will sell for $30.

How to Get Started

Begin marketing with social media, like Facebook, Instagram, and Twitter. When you have a few dollars, create a website. The investment is often less than $50 per year. Use Amazon, eBay, and Etsy to sell products as well. Sometimes it is easier to attract traffic to those sites than to your own website, at least in the beginning. Be sure your photographs are top-notch and that you show the product well enough that someone cannot help but purchase your product. Try to get it into the hands of an influencer (aka famous person), and take photos of them eating your wares.

If the basket or box has multiple items, each one must be at least partially visible. Make it easy for your customer to buy with PayPal, Square, and other credit card order fulfillment services. Payment must be supersimple, or your customer will abandon the purchase halfway through. Look for order fulfillment inside Facebook, for example, rather than making customers click to your website to find the product.

Set yourself apart by looking for items in your town or region that are of interest to visitors or to those who have moved away. Your theme or differentiator may be your locality, a sport, or a values-based point of interest, ranging from ESG (environmental, social, and governance) to vegan culture. Many businesses have sprung up around Second Amendment themes, such as blackriflecoffee.com.

Summarizing the business plan below, I want you to think of this business in three big stages:

Research and marketing. Do your research so that your concept is appealing and people "have to have it." Find ways to market your gifts to your target audience. Use lots of social media for sure, but also look for other ways to connect with your potential customers, such as trade shows or public events, where you can give away samples.

Acquisition and assembly. You will work out a way to make or purchase the contents of your gift baskets and boxes and begin perfecting your presentation. The assembly is important, because the box or basket should arrive without any shifting of the contents, which should look exactly like the picture in your advertisement when the customer opens it. It needs to look awesome upon opening. It's not enough to just get the product to the customer: the presentation has to pop.

Shipping. Half of your work will be packing and shipping these products. Your containers and packing bolsters need to be on point to assure the perfect presentation I mentioned above. This type of packing and shipping is half art and half science. Work out an affordable, effective, and attractive set of materials and methods for good delivery.

So follow me here, y'all. These are great businesses. If you can find some things that people want and like and present and package them in an appealing way, you can create a terrific niche for yourself in the corporate and personal gift space.

Tips and Techniques for Building Your Business

Offer volume discounts for large clients. Perhaps offer 30 percent discount for large bulk orders, but add a 10 percent labor charge to process the order. You will need to adjust these numbers to support your specific overhead and expenses.

Logo and promotional items are a crowded space. Logo pens, water bottles, and coffee mugs are ubiquitous. Enter this space at your own risk—it's very competitive, with too many sellers competing for customers. If you want to succeed in custom logo products, you need to have an incredibly unique offering.

When you do an Internet search of corporate gifts, you will receive over 400 million results. The majority of those are promotional item sellers. Enter this arena at your own risk.

Horizontal Growth

Horizontal growth is easy in this business model. You can continue to innovate the types of products and customer segments you serve. Very Vera created different cakes and pies—all unique, with mouth-watering images. Wine Country Gift Baskets expanded into boxes and tins and then into coffee, chocolate, and snack-themed baskets that do not include wine. In our circle of friends, the coffee gift baskets are the most popular. Finding different price points also helps you grow horizontally, because you are reaching different client segments. For example, a company may send a corporate gift for $150, but a family member is more likely to send a $19 or $29 basket. These are two completely different client segments, almost like two different businesses.

Vertical Growth

The example below—nonprofit subscription boxes—is a great example of vertical growth. They not only sell subscription boxes but manufacture the contents of the boxes in partnership with fair trade craftswomen in Africa. Capturing the manufacturing component of the supply chain is a good vertical.

Variations

Business 96: *Holiday Theme Gifts*

Holiday themes are good if you are willing to have seasonal revenue. The sky is the limit for the combinations you can create for Valentine's Day, Christmas, and other major events.

Business 97: *Location Themes*

I'm from Detroit. There are certain brands and products that are uniquely Detroit: Vernors Ginger Ale, Better Made potato chips, Kellogg's, Sanders candy and fudge, Faygo Pop, and Biggby Coffee. Both Little Caesars and Domino's Pizza (originally DomiNick's) originated in Michigan. My sister Laurie thinks it would be easy to put together a basket or box with some of these Detroit originals that might appeal to corporate gifters and recipients. Imagine a corporation headquartered in Michigan that could send their clients a themed gift that reinforced the giver's roots.

Business 98: *Put It on a Stick*

I don't know why, but people love food on a stick. The original Cookie Bouquet (cookies on sticks arranged in a bouquet) trademark appears to be owned by cookiesbydesign.com and is still popular. What could be better than a bouquet of pastries on sticks? Another of my favorites are cheesecake lollipops—little cheesecake balls dipped in chocolate, rolled in nuts, or drizzled with caramel. Gourmet Gift Baskets offers a gift basket of cheesecake bites

(Cheesecake Lollipops is already trademarked). Edible Arrangements is a franchise creating fresh fruit arrangements that look like flower arrangements. Fruit on a stick.

Many of these franchises claim to be global but do not have a presence in Britain, Europe, Africa, or Asia. I believe there are untapped markets around the world to exploit if you are inspired by some of the incredible innovation and creativity in the American marketplace. In developed markets, let's say London or Berlin, you will need to research the competition and select your niche, although I think many markets are still underserved.

In London, for example, I found only one gift basket and fruit bouquet provider online: Fruity Gift. There are only a few gift basket or gift hamper providers in London, and most of them seem to be local or neighborhood providers. With a population of 9.5 million in metropolitan London, a company styled with true delivery service and online ordering may be able to tap an unmet need.

In developing and emerging markets, you can easily be first to market with an idea and build a dominant business—maybe even franchise your idea. I'm thinking of the emerging wealth I've seen in Manila, Monterrey, Nairobi, and Entebbe. An entrepreneur who carves out a niche, is first to market with an idea, and executes well on that model can quickly build a business in developing and emerging economies. I firmly believe that your growth rate in emerging markets can be much faster than in many developed markets.

Business 99: *Novelty Food Products*

Kermit Carpenter, a disabled veteran, started his side hustle, a smoothie stand in front of Papa's Restaurant in Key West while he was still working as the bookkeeper at Papa's. After Papa's lost its head chef, Kermit was looking for a new gig. While brainstorming with his sister and brother-in-law on a road trip to see his mom, they decided to open Kermit's Key West Key Lime Shoppe. Today they have two locations on Duval Street (Key West's main entertainment strip), one of which is right across from Sunset Pier, as well as another location in DeLand, Florida, with a large fulfillment facility for an exploding Internet sales business. Check them out at KeyLimeShop.com.

One of Kermit's innovations is frozen key lime pie slices, dipped in chocolate, and on a stick for $80 (for twelve bars). My wife, Cheri, drove all the way from Islamorada to buy me a slice one time! This is by far my favorite dessert food. In fact, it may be my favorite food in the whole world! This is a unique, desirable, and lucrative idea. What is your idea?

Business 100: *Subscription Boxes*

The sky's the limit when it comes to possibilities here. Think about all those items that you enjoy, and then put them together in box. Subscription boxes cost the consumer between $10 and $75 per month, depending on what you put in them.

A subscription box is a recurring physical delivery of curated, niche-oriented products packaged in a box designed to create an experience and offer additional value on top of the actual products. It's not just about the products that are being delivered, rather it's about the experience it brings," according to Just4uBox.com. Subscription businesses are called "subcomms" for short.

Bespokepost.com offers themed boxes based on a membership you control. You take a quiz telling them what you like and don't like, and they curate your box. You can preview it, skip it, or keep it. They introduce new options monthly and improve the selections based on subscribers' feedback. Cost is $45 per month. This is the ultimate fulfillment of my foundational principle, "Give people what they want."

Another example is FabFitFun, one of the top subscription boxes for women, which offers a quarterly subscription for $49.99. Included in the box are wellness, skin care, and lifestyle products, often worth four times the subscription cost. This keeps subscribers eagerly waiting for the next shipment. Alltrue (formerly CAUSE-BOX) contains products from socially conscious companies. Items include jewelry, home decor, gifts, and more. Subscriptions for this are $54.95 per quarter.

You could assemble a collection of men's items, dog toys and accessories, food items, clothing, jewelry, holiday decorating items, wine, collectibles and crafts, and much more. To find products, it's easy to do research online. For handmade items, Etsy is the place to go. Perhaps there is someone in your town or city whose craftmanship or culinary artistry you admire. Approach them, and begin a collaboration. The key here is to sell what appeals to you. This will make it easier to spread the word about your offerings. Lucky Tackle Box, which offers bait and other fishing paraphernalia, is one I've watched launch and build an audience on Instagram.

My favorite subscription box story is about a couple I met at a train-the-trainer event for entrepreneurial school. They traveled to Africa on a short trip with Compassion International, which provides help to women who are victims of trafficking. The couple decided to support the nonprofit by helping build a transition home to which the girls could escape and learn how to reenter society with the dignity of financial independence. They began training and supporting the girls as they created jewelry and clothing for sale on a fair-trade website.

The sales did not keep up with the supply of goods, and the business enterprise had to be subsidized by the nonprofit and donors. So they turned to a subscription box model, offering a surprise collection of fair-trade goods, such as jewelry, sandals, and scarves, that would arrive in a box to the subscriber each month. The idea was a huge hit. Not only were they able to balance their inventory by selling collections, they were able to find their X-factor: connecting with their audience spiritually.

The last time I heard from them, the service had over 3,000 subscribers at $32.99 per month. That is roughly $100,000 in gross revenue per month, equaling $1.2 million annually. And 100 percent of the profits go to the girls! All of this from the garage of their Texas home. Check out MercyHouseGlobal.org and the subscription site: FairtTadeFriday.club.

How to Get Started

Like with many other businesses, a lot can be done for a little bit of time by posting to social media. As time goes on and you have a little cash to invest in marketing, social media influencers will endorse your product for a fee, including "stars" on Instagram or bloggers who write product endorsements. Be sure they have a significant number of followers before turning your hard-earned cash over to them. Create a website as well. This too is fairly simple and inexpensive.

18

Marketing Products for Others through Direct Sales

Opportunities come infrequently. When it rains gold,
put out the bucket, not the thimble.
—WARREN BUFFETT

In direct sales, you sell products to consumers online, at home, work, shows, parties, or other nonstore locations. The Direct Selling Association (dsa.org) says:

> Direct selling is a business model that offers entrepreneurial opportunities to individuals as independent contractors to market and/or sell products and services, typically outside of a fixed retail establishment, through one-to-one selling, in-home product demonstrations or online. Compensation is ultimately based on sales and may be earned based on personal sales and/or the sales of others in their sales organizations.
>
> Direct sellers may be called distributors, representatives, consultants, or various other titles. They may participate in various ways, including selling the products themselves or through their sales organizations, providing training and leadership to

their sales organizations, referring customers to the company and purchasing products and services for personal use.

Business 101:
Floor Sweeper to Owner in One Year

After college, Dale found himself working the graveyard shift, 10:00 p.m. to 5:00 a.m., sweeping floors at a twenty-four-hour diner for less than minimum wage. A patron invited him to daywork swinging a sledgehammer on a demolition and remodeling of an office supply store. He took the second job and was sleeping three hours a day.

The customers at the office supply store thought it was entertaining to watch Dale pounding away at the double brick wall. After a few minutes, they would ask something like, "Young man, do you know where the copy paper is?" Sledgehammer in hand, Dale would walk them over a few aisles and help them carry out their case of paper. He was so helpful that after the remodel, the owner asked him to stay on, sweeping floors and unloading boxcars full of office furniture for minimum wage.

A few months later, Dale was offered a higher-paying job as a landman, buying natural gas leases in West Texas. But shortly after, he discovered that he had two detached retinas and ended up on his back for a multiweek recovery from surgery. To his surprise, his former boss from the office supply company came to visit him. "I've hired five people to do your job, and they still can't get it done. I want you to come back when you've recovered," the business owner told him.

"I can't afford to work for you at minimum wage," Dale told his former employer.

"I don't want you to come back as an employee," the business-man said. "I want you to come back as my partner."

**Do your minimum wage job so well that
your boss can't afford to be without you.**

Dale couldn't believe what he was hearing. "I want to open two new stores, and you will be my partner in them," concluded the owner. In less than ten years, the businesses were grossing $3.5 million a year, and Dale had bought out his former boss.

Today the traditional office supply business is gone, gobbled up by Office Depot, Sam's Club, and others; however, Dale has established himself as the preeminent provider of office furniture, designing, selling, and installing offices and cubicle farms in Fortune 500 companies, new factories, and government projects. He utilizes a direct sales model, selling from the white-labeled web pages and catalogs provided by his buying group (more on that below) and manufacturers. With this model, he does not need the money to maintain a massive inventory to meet his orders.

How to Get Started

You can begin by researching companies that provide products or services that you find interesting, or something else that relates to your experience, areas of interest, or skillset. Research those companies to narrow your list to the top three. Then perform your due diligence to pick one that is reputable, has a good record of success with its partners, and you are excited to sell. If you wouldn't sell it to family and friends, don't select that opportunity.

Nothing is as important as passion. No matter what you want to do with your life, be passionate.   —Jon Bon Jovi

Let's take a look at Dale's business—Office Furniture USA. If you want to start a business like his, you can join the Independent Suppliers Group (ISG), a group of office products dealers who believe that a cooperative effort with other independent dealers provides the best opportunity for success. ISG members are locally owned businesses that utilize shared merchandising and marketing resources as well as manufacturer relationships. Their mission statement: "ISG empowers its members with purchasing programs, sales, and marketing tools and leverages the combined size, strength, knowledge, and experience so its members can succeed in their marketplace." Joining a group like this arms you with the office furniture catalog and dealer's account, from which you can solicit furniture orders from customers, place those orders, and receive shipments.

You will collect 50 percent down payment with your client's order and the balance upon delivery, so you don't need a pile of cash to maintain inventory or float orders. The manufacturer will provide payment terms called *net 15* or *net 30*, which means you will collect from your client and remit your final payment to the manufacturer in less than 15 or 30 days. Most offer a 1 percent credit or rebate if you pay in less than 10 days.

In addition, the manufacturers have sophisticated space planning departments that will prepare, on your behalf, the blueprint for your customer's space, showing all of the cubicles and furniture arranged within the client's location. This level of support from the network and manufacturer (which didn't exist a few years ago) enables you to deliver a high degree of professionalism to your customers, even though you are not beginning your business with a ton of experience in the industry.

Marketing

As with many businesses, networking and social media are going to be your best tools for meeting potential customers.

Networking is easy and usually costs nothing. Here are three simple, low-cost networking opportunities:

- Business mixers, open houses, and ribbon cuttings are easy to find online or in the newspaper—they're free, fun, and full of people. Your local chamber of commerce and other community organizations will regularly announce open houses (like a Christmas open house hosted by a business), grand openings, grand reopenings, and ribbon cuttings, which are often open to the public. You should attend dressed appropriately, which means, look great! Don't overdress or underdress, but always look like a professional. Depending on the type of business you start, a logo shirt may be appropriate, but not always in good taste. Organizations like the Rotary Club may fine you $1 for wearing a logo shirt! They understand that your peers will respect you more for being a good neighbor and volunteer than for handing out your business card like a Vegas blackjack dealer.

- Volunteer and civic associations and nonprofits. Rule number one for your interaction with these groups is never, ever, solicit your peers. Don't worry: people will ask what you do for a living or what business you are engaged in. The most important thing here (and in the next category: religious and special interest groups) is that you dedicate yourself to being the best volunteer or group member that you can be. Spend your time being selfless, helpful, and kind to others. In time, people will want to support you in whatever business you are in and will seek you out. If you are self-centered, insincere, and oversolicitous, people will shun you. Be yourself, be awesome, and your business will grow to be a respected part of your community.

P.S. Even if yours is an online business, you will succeed best when you build a community of like-minded people who respect and appreciate you in your virtual online world.

- Church, synagogue, mosque, and social or special interest clubs and associations. Follow rule number one above: never, ever, solicit your brothers, sisters, and pals from these circles. Seek first that which God has called you to be as a person. Be yourself. Live your calling fully as a person, a brother, sister, father, son, volunteer, citizen, neighbor, or friend and you will find that success in business will follow you. You won't be able to escape it. Be the best person you can be, and let your business follow your life well lived.

Social media is the most powerful tool that you can employ in your business to connect with customers and potential customers. Numerous studies on marketing tools cited social media as the number one tool utilized by the most successful companies in America. The key here is to provide value with useful information on a consistent basis on your platforms—whether it be Twitter, LinkedIn, Instagram, Facebook. (See business 80 above to see how Sew with Joe rocked it with Facebook.)

Tips and Techniques for Building Your Business

Work hard, even if you don't make a lot of money at first. Dale told me he made $15,000 in his first year. I replied, "You worked cheap."

He responded, "I wasn't in it for the money. I wanted to build something."

"I wasn't in it for the money. I wanted to build something."

Be cautious with multilevel marketing (MLM) and pyramid marketing schemes. They can be great money-making vehicles if you are on the first or second level, coming in immediately at the inception of the company. If you are coming into the program downline, you have a high probability of losing money, especially if you include your time in the calculation. The enticing stories of success you hear are most often from or about the people at the top of the pyramid.

My biggest concern here is the opportunity cost. I've watched friends and acquaintances invest years of sincere effort into MLM businesses and find little success. The same passion, dedication, and time investment would yield huge results in a hundred other start-ups or ventures.

Multilevel Marketing

Did I mention that I mistrust MLM? I do, but for some this might be a good side gig. If you find this type of opportunities attractive, remember to base your income and success projections on the product you can sell, not on the downline you can build (unless, again, you are at the first or second level in a new company). If it is a mature business, your ability to build a downline of other associates is limited by the current market saturation. Everyone has already heard the pitch. The end result for many is simply that you, your family, and friends become consumers of the products rather than viable recruiters or resellers. Be careful. Enter at your own risk.

Here are a few of the most popular MLM companies. I'm including the year they were founded and the resale volume in dollars, so you can consider the market saturation of these opportunities: Amway, 1959, $8.8 billion; Avon, 1886, $5.7 billion; Herbalife, 1980, $4.5 billion; Natura, 1969, $4.4 billion; Mary Kay, 1963, $3.5 billion; Nu Skin, 1984, $2.2 billion; Tupperware, 1948, $2.26 billion; Melaleuca, 1985, $2 billion; Primerica, 1977, $1.6 billion; Young Living, 1993, $1.5 billion; Ambit Energy, 2006, $1.1 billion; Shaklee, 1956, $84 million.

Partial List of Direct Sales Companies

I haven't vetted this list, nor am I endorsing any of the companies. It includes MLM businesses. You will need to evaluate each opportunity and perform your due diligence to determine if it is a good opportunity for you.

- 4Life Research, LLC. Nutritional products and supplements
- Abby + Anna. Leggings, tunics, and dresses for women and young girls
- AdvoCare International. Nutritional and skin care products
- Agnes & Dora. Comfy leggings, tunics, and dresses that are made in the USA.
- Aihu. Healing skin care and body products
- Alice's Table. Hosting floral arrangement parties. They claim that you will take home up to 70 percent of ticket sales (before the cost of flowers) and can earn up to $600 per two-hour event. You can also earn mentoring bonuses.
- All Dazzle. Jewelry
- Aloette Cosmetics, Inc. Good-for-your-skin skin care and makeup
- Amway-Quixtar. Health and wellness products

- Angelamoore.com. Jewelry
- Arbonne International. Botanically based beauty and health-care products
- Avon. Bath and beauty products, clothing, and jewelry
- Azuli Skye. Jewelry
- Barefoot Books. Award-winning children's books, CDs, and gifts
- beFragrant. Candles, melts, body sprays, and more
- BeachBody. Workout videos and home fitness programs
- Beauty Counter. Chic, safe, and effective beauty products
- Beauty Society. Skin care and beauty products
- Become. Anti-aging cosmeceutical skin care products
- Black Box Cosmetics. Bath, body, and skin care products
- Body Wise. Meal replacement shakes and nutritional products
- Boisset Collection. Wine, jewelry, accessories, and gifts
- bon Cook. Cooking and baking supplies
- cabi. High-end, stylish clothing by Carol Anderson
- Carico. Fine china, cutlery, tableware, and crystal
- Carlisle Collection. High-end fashion for women
- Celadon Road. Natural, ecofriendly products for everyday needs
- Celebratinghome.com. Home products
- Chalky & Company. All-natural chalk paint
- CharleeJack. Hosts custom painting parties.
- Close to My Heart. Scrapbooking supplies and products
- Cocoa Exchange. Premium chocolate treats and products
- Color Street. Nail designs and applications
- Compelling Creations, Inc. Inspirational jewelry
- Cookielee.com. Jewelry
- Creative Memories. Scrapbooking products and supplies

- Crowned Free. A Christian-based company that sells women's clothing, accessories, and jewelry
- CUTCO. Cutlery
- Damsel in Defense. Self-defense products for women
- DeTech. Fire safety equipment
- Discovery Toys. Educational toys
- Do You Bake? Gourmet mixes, dips, spices, and more
- doTERRA. Essential oils
- Dudley Beauty Corp. Hair care, cosmetics, skin care, products for men, and gifts
- Ellie Kai. Made-to-order clothing for women and little girls
- Epicure Selections. Mealtime solutions for the home chef
- Esbe Designs. Handcrafted jewelry designed by Sara Blaine
- Essential Bodywear. Bras, panties, and shapewear
- Etcetera. Women's clothing
- EVER. Botanically-based skin care products. A Stella & Dot family brand
- F.A.I.T.H. A Christian-based company that sells jewelry
- fibi & clo. Shoes and accessories
- Fifth Avenue Collection. Beautiful jewelry; an international company
- Forever Living. Health, wellness, and weight loss products, as well as essential oils
- For Tails Only. Gourmet pet treats and products
- Forever Green. Natural energy drinks
- Fuller Brush Company. Cleaning brushes
- Fundanoodle. Early education products for children
- Gold Canyon. Candles and fragrances for the home
- Grace & Heart. Faith-inspired jewelry
- Grace Wear Collections. Jewelry, purses, and accessories

- H2O at Home. Natural home care products, organic personal care products, and natural home fragrance
- HealthyJointsSkin. Joint discomfort relief/anti-aging
- Harpers Love. Trendy personalized jewelry
- Hello Pink. Clothing for women, kids, maternity, and men
- Heritage Makers. Scrapbooking supplies and products
- I Thought of You. Fair trade jewelry and handmade goods
- In a Pikle. Compact organizers for essential convenience items needed for life's emergencies
- Initial Outfitters. Christian-inspired direct sales company that offers personalized gifts and jewelry
- Initials, Inc. Monogrammed totes, bags, purses, wallets, luggage, and storage containers
- Isagenix. Healthy weight loss products
- It Works. Body wraps
- J. Hilburn. Stylish men's clothing
- Jafra. Cosmetics and beauty products
- Java Momma. Organic fair trade coffee, flavored coffee, loose leaf tea, cocoa, and accessories
- Jerky Direct. Beef jerky
- Jeunesse Global. Wellness products
- Jewel Scent. Candles and bath bombs with hidden jewelry inside
- Jewelry Candles. Candles with hidden jewelry inside
- Jordan Essentials. Bath and body products for adults and children
- Just Jewelry. A Christian-based company selling jewelry
- Kaeser & Blair. Promotional products
- KEEP Collective. One of a kind bracelets and necklaces that can be personalized; a Stella & Dot family brand

- Kilambe Coffee. Gourmet organic coffee
- Kirby. Vacuums and bags, replacement parts, and cleaning products
- Kyani. Superfood juice
- La Señorita Jolie. Clothing and jewelry
- Labella Baskets. Gift baskets
- L'BRI Pure N' Natural. Natural Aloe Vera skin care products
- Le-Vel. Wellness supplements
- Life Force. Nutritional supplements
- Linen World. Home decor, linens, toys, organizational solutions, and more
- Lusomé. Luxury sleepwear that keeps women cool when sleeping
- Llynda More. Interchangeable boots, sandals, and accessories
- Magnabilities. Customized magnetic jewelry
- Magnolia and Vine. Customizable jewelry and accessories
- Makeup Eraser. Chemical-free makeup removal towel
- Mannatech. Nutritional supplements
- Martha and Mary. Christian-inspired direct sales company that offers a blend of business and ministry, selling home decor items and gifts
- Mary Kay. Cosmetics, skin and body products
- Maskcara Beauty. Makeup
- Matilda Jane Clothing. Children's and women's clothing
- Melaleuca. Personal care, cosmetics, cleaning, and wellness products
- Metrin. Skin care products
- Mia Bella. Candles and melts
- Modicare. Laundry, auto, and personal and home care products
- MONAT Global. All-natural hair care products

- Morinda. Essential oils, noni juice, skin care products, and lip products
- My Pan Party. Kitchenware and supplies
- Nature's Sunshine. Health and wellness products
- Ndulge. Leggings, both casual and activewear, for women and little girls
- Nerium International. Science-based skin care products
- Nikken. Wellness products
- Noevir. Skin care, hair care, body care, and cosmetics
- Noonday Collections. Jewelry and accessories
- Norwex. Environmentally friendly cleaning products and personal care products
- NuSkin. Skin care products
- Nygard Style. Women's clothing (pants, jackets, and shirts) with patented SLIM Curve technology, which lifts, shapes, and sculpts your figure
- Nyla and Noelle. Women's leggings, wraps, dresses, jumpsuits, shirts, and jewelry
- NYR Organic. Organic hair care, body, cosmetics, aromatherapy, herbal remedies, and more
- One Hope. Wine, gifts, and other gourmet products company that also provides built-in donations to various charities
- Origami Owl. Personalized charm jewelry
- Pampered Chef. Kitchenware and gifts
- Paparazzi Jewelry. Jewelry for $5
- Park Lane Jewelry. Jewelry
- Part & Parcel. Clothing for plus-sized women
- PartyLite. Candles, home decor, and gifts
- pawTree. Pet food seasonings, food, treats, supplements, and accessories

- Pink Zebra. Candles and home fragrances
- Peach. Clothing, accessories, and undergarments for gym, work, and play
- Peekaboo Beans. Children's clothing
- PeoplesWay. Wellness products
- Perfectly Posh. Pampering products
- Pierre Lang. Designer jewelry
- P!phany. Leggings, dresses, skirts, tunics, cardigans, pants, and T-shirts for women
- Plexus. All-natural, healthy solutions to help individuals lose weight
- Plumeria Bath. Bath bombs, soaps, beauty products, and gifts
- Plunder. Vintage-style jewelry at savvy prices
- Premier Designs. Christian-inspired company that sells jewelry
- Princess House. Products for your home
- Pure Haven Essentials. Safe personal care products
- Purely. Essential oils, beauty products, products for men, and jewelry
- Rainbow. Home cleaning systems
- RBC Life Sciences. Nutritional supplements and natural personal care products
- Red Aspen. Lashes, lip and nail products
- Regal Ware Worldwide. Cookware
- Reliv. Nutritional products
- Rena Ware. Cookware, juicers and water purifiers
- Restaurant.com. Business-to-business (B2B) opportunity where independent consultants get local restaurants to participate in daily offerings
- Rodan + Fields. Dermatology-based skin care treatments for men, women, and teens

- Royal Prestige. Cookware
- Ruby Ribbon. Clothes with built-in shapewear
- Saba. Appetite control and energy supplements
- Sabika. Jewelry
- Saladmaster. Complete cooking systems
- Scentsy. Wickless candles
- Scout & Cellar. Wine
- SendOutCards. Personalized greeting cards and invitations online. Prints, stuffs, and mails them, all for less than the price of a greeting card at the store.
- SeneGence International. Long-lasting cosmetics
- Shaklee.com. Wellness products
- Signature Homestyles. Home decor and interior products
- Silver Icing. Chic and comfy clothes
- SimplyFun. Play products (board games, family games, and party games) that bring families and friends together
- Simply Said Designs. Home decor
- Smart Living Company. Home decor, lighting, and outdoor living products
- Soul Purpose. Bath and body products
- Sportron International Inc. Wellness products
- SQN Sport. Women's activewear made in the USA.
- Sseko Designs. An ethical fashion brand that sells apparel, sandals, jewelry, handbags, and accessories that benefit women in Uganda through a work program that enables them to attend university
- Stampin' Up! Rubber stamps and accessories
- Steeped Tea. Loose tea, gourmet mixes, and other kitchen and food accessories
- Stella & Dot. Jewelry, clothing, bags, charms, and accessories

- Style Dots. Jewelry
- Sunrider. Health and beauty products
- Surepets.com. Pet products
- Sweet Minerals. All-natural, mineral-based makeup and skin care products
- SwissJust Corporation. Natural Swiss products for body and mind
- Tastefully Simple. Gourmet foods and gifts
- Taste of Gourmet. Gourmet food products
- Tealightful Treasures. Gourmet teas and food mixes
- The Gourmet Cupboard. Gourmet food mixes and coffee
- Thirty-One. Christian-inspired company that sells bags, totes, purses, and backpacks
- Threads Worldwide. Fair trade handcrafted jewelry and accessories
- Thrive Life. Food, seasonings, sauces, snacks, beverages, and more
- Tocara. Fine jewelry
- Tori Belle. Magnetic eyeliner, lashes, and makeup
- Touchstone Crystal. Swarovski crystal-embellished jewelry
- Traci Lynn Fashion Jewelry. Affordable fashion jewelry
- Tracy Negoshian. Clothing
- Trades of Hope. Fair trade jewelry made by artisans from around the world
- Traveling Vineyard. Wine
- TruAura. Makeup
- Tristar. Air purifiers
- TriVita. Herbs and nutritional supplements
- Tula Xii. Customizable lifestyle organizers
- Tupperware. Storage solutions

- Unicity International. Nutritional, personal care, and wellness products
- USANA. Nutritional and personal care products
- Usborne Books and More. Children's books
- Valentus. Health and vitality supplements and drinks
- Vantel Pearls in the Oyster. Pearls
- VIC Cosmetics. Makeup
- ViSalus. Weight loss and fitness products
- VOXXLife. Socks with Voxx HPT technology for wellness
- W by Worth. Clothing for women
- Watkins Online. Home care and personal care items
- Wildtree. Natural gourmet culinary blends, infused grape-seed oils, dressings, and sauces
- Willing Beauty. Healthy skin care products and makeup for twentysomethings
- Willow House. Home and party products
- Wine Shop at Home. Wine
- Wink Kitten. Fake eyelashes
- Yanbal. Makeup, skin care products, and jewelry
- YOR Health. Nutritional products and supplements
- Young Living. Essential oils
- Youngevity. Wellness and health products, beauty and care products, and food and beverage products
- Younique. Makeup and accessories
- Zermat International. Skin care, body care, and makeup
- Zija. Essential oils
- Zrii. Liquid nutritional supplements
- ZYMBOL. Inspirational jewelry based on a design element that contains every letter and every number, hidden in an intricate design

Horizontal Growth

Horizontal or organic growth for these businesses will include reaching new clients with your existing products and/or selling more products to your existing customers. You can accomplish this by bringing additional sales representatives into your organization and duplicating your sales success through others. The great thing about this is that you are helping others while you grow your business—it's the magic of free markets.

In addition, you may want to expand by representing a second or third manufacturer. If you are independently representing an office furniture manufacturer, it's not difficult to represent two or three manufacturers at the same time. You will be able to offer a wider range of products and perhaps attract new or different client segments.

Vertical Growth

If you want to grow your direct sales business vertically or strategically, you can manufacture, wholesale, deliver, and/or assemble the products you are currently selling.

Manufacture. We've looked at businesses that sell custom soap, jewelry, and custom clothing. They have fairly low barriers to entry. Let's talk about soap: if you are selling health and beauty products today, you may introduce your own line of soap (see the profile of OutlawSoaps.com above). Customers who are currently buying beauty products that you are selling on behalf of a manufacturer may be candidates for your brand of beauty product.

Wholesale. If you find success retailing a product, for example jewelry imported from an exotic location, you may be able to expand into wholesaling these products to other retailers. You can grow that business through B2B trade shows, which are easily found online at sites like WholesaleCentral.com. Perennial locations such as the DallasMarketCenter.com claim to be complete wholesale trade resource centers. You can become an exhibitor and reach more than 200,000 buyers (buying inventory for their retail business) in a single location. Check out the details at http://dallasmarketcenter .com/leasing/gettingstarted. Most major metropolitan areas have similar permanent or temporary markets, where retail businesses buy inventory from wholesalers, suppliers, and manufacturers.

Transportation, delivery, and assembly. You may find vertical growth by transporting or importing your products, such as exotic jewelry. With office furniture sales, you may find that delivering the merchandise and assembling it for the customer is a complementary service to the sale of the furniture.

19

Guide to Website, Online Store, and Virtual Office Tools for Online Commerce

In our rapidly changing world, I believe frequent reinventing yourself is safer than doing things you've always done.
—STEVE BOOKBINDER, CEO OF DIGITAL MEDIA TRAINING

Every business needs a website. At least I can't think of a business that doesn't, and website fumbles are the most frequent mistakes I see startup entrepreneurs make.

If you're starting a business with little to no money, you will want to go with the solutions I recommended in business 5 related to blogging.

One of the best places to start is WordPress.org (not WordPress .com). Word Press is the most popular way to make a blog or website, according to W3Techs. The difference is that WordPress.org requires you to self-host, which means you'll need to add the hosting for $3–$6 per month at the likes of DreamHost, Bluehost, or GoDaddy. You will have thousands of free themes and tens of thousands of free plug-ins, like eCommerce and contact forms. You don't need any technical knowledge to set it up, and you will own your content and data. Have fun setting up your look and theme!

Website Mistakes to Avoid

Multipage website. Yes, I know what you're going to say: your website should be deep and wide with tons of content and pages. But for our purposes here, I want you to get your website up fast and clean—and for very little cost. For most small businesses, especially at the beginning, your web page is not creating original traffic and unique new customers. Instead, the prospective customers you are generating through social media, networking, or grassroots marketing are going to your web page to validate their decision to contact you or buy from you. In the old days, if you were going to buy a bicycle, you would look up bicycles in the Yellow Pages, find an address for a listing that appealed to you (maybe influenced by the name or a display ad), then drive to the store. You would eyeball the front of the store before going in. You would ask, is it clean, in a safe neighborhood? Is the sign bright clear and illuminated? Is the storefront inviting? Are their bicycles parked out front? If you liked the look of the place, you would go in.

Today your website is your storefront. social media, Etsy, eBay, Amazon, and Shopify are like the Yellow Pages. People are more likely to find you in those channels than through your website—in the early stages of your business. As your business matures, you'll master the art of search engine optimization (SEO) and drive original views and visits to your site. For now, you just need a clean, professional, inviting landing page that makes people comfortable buying from your eBay or Etsy store or to purchase professional services from you. Don't forget: when it comes to customers validating their intention to buy from you, your Google listing may be as important as your web page.

"My website has to be perfect." This is one of the hardest things for me to watch. A person decides to launch a business and puts the website at the end of the to-do list. Then, once they begin the website project, they hire a website guru and spend the next six to twelve months fussing over what word goes where, which picture to use here, what icon to use there. They launch the business with no web page presence. Don't make that mistake. Decide on your story, your value proposition. State it in one or two sentences at the top of your web page. It could be this simple: "Get your time back. Devon Smith: virtual assistant," or "Feel the sand between your toes: Mahalo Fashion Accessories." Look at Shopify's landing page—it's just ten words: "Sell online with Shopify: trusted by over 1,000,000 businesses worldwide," followed by a call to action box, where the prospect fills in their email address and presses the button that says, "Get Started." It's that simple—keep it simple.

Make that message about the prospective client. Sell the sizzle, not the steak.

Have a clear, concise call to action, such as "Click here to go to my online store" or "Call me at (555) 555-5555."

Use the blog feature to post daily or weekly messages, testimonies from happy customers, or inspiring photos (your clothing worn by a happy person on a sailboat, or a satisfied customer with your product).

That's all you need to get started. As your business matures, your website will mature, with more content. You'll refine the message, you'll optimize search, and you'll improve the design over time—but don't worry; it doesn't need to be perfect on day one. I'm not recommending that you put up a sloppy web page. I'm saying, keep it simple in the beginning, and get it going in one day.

Too much salesy jargon. Don't load up the page with "we, we, we": "We offer this, we offer that." Focus your short, simple message on the benefit your customer will derive from your product or service, and leave it there. Save the lengthy explanations for your content marketing, such as your blog and social media posts, which will educate, inform, and entertain your prospects with good words, posts, articles, videos, and images.

Not enough value-added content. As I've already written, keep your value proposition—your story—short and sweet. Use the blog on your site to post value-added content, that is, material that goes above and beyond. If your business is as a dog trainer, provide tips and techniques related to dogs on your blog and social media. If you provide mobile facials, then offer skin care solutions that can be done at home between facials. As a wealth advisor, I provided articles informing people about topics like how to prepare for tax season, how to roll over a 401(k) from a former employer, or addressing questions like, "Should I open a Roth IRA?"

The "About Us" page. Forget the "About Us" tab on your website, because it's really about the customer! Make your messaging revolve around the benefits customers will derive from your product or service. How will it make them feel? How will it solve their problem? Will it meet their need? People do indeed want to know about you, and as I've written earlier, you are your brand. If you're a sole proprietor, put your bio right on the landing page, with a good picture. Don't put a lame photo on your web page. Do whatever it takes to obtain a great photo—don't skimp on this!

Oops! Forgot about the Google listing. I get a lot of pushback on this topic, because many people think a Google My Business listing is not important—but it is. It enables your business to appear in local search results for queries specific to your products or services. Even broad queries with large search volumes display local results in the three advertisements at the top of the results page, and small business owners can capitalize on this.

Here's an example of a business I randomly queried. I lived in Westchester County, north of New York City, and fell in love with Sal's Pizza in Mamaroneck. I haven't been there for more than twenty years, so just for kicks, I thought I would do two common Google queries for my old pizza-by-the-slice joint—one that a typical potential customer might do.

First, I searched for "pizza, Mamaroneck," and my result set, below the three advertisements at the top, was the Google search result summary box, two Yelp listings, a TripAdvisor ad, followed by Sal's actual website. The Google summary box includes three pizzerias with my old fave, Sal's, at the top, sporting 4.6 stars. If you click on Sal's in the summary box, the view changes, and Sal's full Google My Business listing opens on top of the map in the center of the page. If Sal's did not have the Google My Business listing, their listing with details (hours, address, phone number) would not appear.

The second query is a direct search for the business itself: "Sal's Pizza, Mamaroneck, NY." My search result now returns Sal's Google My Business listing on the right side of the page, Sal's actual website at the top left of the page, and some great video reviews in the video scroller below their website link. If you do the same search on mobile, the entire screen is filled with Sal's Google My Business listing (not their own website). This page includes the star ratings, icons for one-touch calling, directions, bookmark, and one-click to their website. The address, map, and hours are below, along with the menu. This is an essential part of you web presence for almost any business. Be sure you spend the time to get it right, and keep the information current.

In order to get started, just search for "How do I create my Google Business Profile?"

Failing to monetize your business idea. Your sale is only complete when the money is in your hand. After all of your planning, creativity, and marketing is done, you now need a way to facilitate the sale of your product or service and receive payment. In other words, how do your customers actually buy from you, and how do you get paid?

In a traditional business, your customer would hand you paper money, a check, or a plastic credit card. In the virtual world, you will take payments online. Your customers will usually pay you with a credit card number, expiration date, and code. You may also choose to accept alternative methods of payment from the likes of PayPal or Apple Pay. I have both but find that many customers do not have PayPal or Apple Pay and prefer to provide a traditional credit card number. Start your business with traditional credit card payment, and then add PayPal or Apple Pay. Don't start with PayPal alone, or you'll alienate some buyers.

Business: Exchange of Value

All business is an exchange of value. You will provide a product or a service, and your customer will exchange value (almost always money) for that product or service. In this section, I'm going to divide sales into two categories:

1. Sale of products
2. Sale of services

The sale of a *product* will include the types of tools with which you are probably already familiar, such as an online store, a shopping cart on your website, an eBay store, or similar online venues where customers can buy your products.

The sale of *services* is different. It may include detailed descriptions, demos, and videos, but ultimately you are providing a service (or perhaps a digital deliverable, like a transcript) rather than a physical product.

If you are selling a product, you can build a store on your own website, and/or you can utilize third-party sites and services to sell online. Many of the virtual third-party stores are like opening your own little storefront—except that these are virtual and online. Using templates provided by these vendors, you can be up and running very quickly. Another advantage of these third-party selling partners, like Amazon and eBay, is searchability. You need people—lots of them—to find you online. When you build your own website and offer products or services on it, the masses may have trouble finding you. By contrast, it is easy for potential customers to find your products on Etsy, Amazon, or eBay. Search engines like Google will not likely place your website at the top of the list of search results.

When you take an online partner like Amazon, eBay, and Etsy, it may be easier for customers to find you online, because Amazon and Etsy are optimizing the search results. They're even paying Google to push search results on their site to the top of the list. If you are selling estate jewelry on your website and also on eBay, then go to your search engine, type in the exact description of the item, for example, "Amethyst set in platinum." Nine times out of ten, you will find that the top search engine results will be eBay, Etsy, Amazon, and Pinterest.

I just tried it. I typed "Amethyst set in platinum" into the Google search bar, and my results were one retailer of new amethyst jewelry, gemvara.com, and then Etsy.com, eBay.com, and Amazon.com, in that order. The first private website of a retailer was midway down on the second page of search results: treosrmontecito.com, a significant reseller and retailer. As a startup, without significant investment in search optimization, you may find yourself five or ten pages deep into search results, which may not generate the quantity of traffic and buyers to your site that you need to hit your goals.

Shopify versus Etsy: Shopify is an e-commerce platform, while Etsy is a marketplace. Shopify has great sales tools, is extremely scalable, and helps you build a great online store, but does not bring you a marketplace. You have to create your own traffic. Etsy does not provide robust storefront capabilities, but has great exposure, with millions of customers shopping on Etsy, then finding your brand.

Using virtual storefront and retailing partners can help you get the most exposure, simplify the startup process, and give you a venue, sometimes multiple venues, to sell your product. Here are some of the most common selling partners.

Amazon is one of the oldest seller's marketplaces. Amazon's selling account charges 99 cents per item, for up to 40 items per month, plus percentage fees depending on the category in which your item appears. Professional selling accounts, with over 40 items, incur a $39.99 monthly fee. If you want the biggest audience, Amazon is the most visited e-commerce property in the United States. In June 2021, they had over 2.7 billion visits.

eBay pioneered online selling in 1995. You'll pay a listing fee plus category fees for your item to appear in other categories, as well as a percentage of the final sale and shipping fees. eBay's traffic is huge, with 182 million active buyers; however, it is generally less trusted than Amazon.

Shopify.com may be one of the easiest and most user-friendly sites to sell your products on. For only $29 per month, Shopify will provide you with your own website, blog, SSL certificates, social media sales channels, and abandoned shopping cart recovery, among other tools. With great customer service, Shopify also integrates well with other third-party apps.

Etsy.com. Buyers spent over $3 billion on Etsy last year on art, collectibles, handmade goods, and antiques. Etsy is one of the easiest sites to use and charges 20 cents to list an item for four months; then it charges 5 percent transaction + 3 percent + 25 cents transaction charge once you sell an item. Etsy processes all your transactions, so you don't need to set up payment processing separately. They also have a 15 percent offsite advertising program. Go to etsy.com/sell.

RubyLane.com. The EcommerceBytes 2019 survey voted Ruby Lane as the number one recommended selling venue. They receive more than a million unique visitors every month and are known by enthusiasts for vintage and antique products. You pay a $100 setup fee and $69 per month for 80 items or less. If vintage and antique is your niche, Ruby Lane may be your venue.

Charish.com is an online consignment store focusing on high quality furniture and home decor. Listings are free. Charish takes a percentage of the sale, beginning at 20 percent for the first $2,500, with the percentage going down by breakpoints to 3 percent as the price goes up.

Facebook Marketplace, Craigslist, and Nextdoor help you sell your goods locally, often for local pickup rather than for shipping, as is common with the sales models I've listed above. It's supereasy to get started: just snap a couple of photos and post your item. You can set up a seller's account in about ten minutes.

Nextdoor is new to me but appears to be growing rapidly. This sales platform is free and is regarded as a little safer than Craigslist because it requires you to create an account.

Most of your neighbors are posting what appear to be deliberately ugly photos to Facebook Marketplace, Craigslist, and Nextdoor, so you can dominate these venues by posting crisp, clear photos and precise, thorough descriptions of your products. For most products, your photos should show all sides and have solid white or black backgrounds. Highlight damages and blemishes, so people know you're a straight shooter and a reputable seller.

OfferUp and **letgo** offer both an online and mobile app presence. The recent merger of these two companies is expected to make a big impact in the online selling arena. "The acquisition will see two of the largest third-party buying and selling marketplaces—outside of Craigslist, eBay, and Facebook Marketplace of course, become a more significant threat to the incumbents," reports Sarah Perez in an article on Tech Crunch. "Together, the new entity will have more than 20 million monthly active users across the US For consumers, the deal means they'll no longer have to list in as many apps when looking to unload some household items, electronics, furniture or whatever else they want to sell."

WebsiteBuilderExpert.com is a good place to visit for terrific articles and drill-downs comparing many of these tools and deeper-dive comparisons, instructions, reviews, and guidance.

Secondary Support

Here are some companies that provide secondary support in the twenty-first century virtual marketplace.

Oberlo lets you find products, add them to your Shopify store, and ship them directly to your customers. No inventory. You can start drop-shipping almost immediately. If you are not creating your own products, you can resell products built on a theme or a niche, like pink flamingos and turtle jewelry for an island theme, or maybe you prefer a golf theme. Find your niche.

Spend a little time to think through this drop-ship concept.

You can simply search on Oberlo or the companies below for products that you want to sell, but you don't have to order any inventory or spend any money on product and samples. Simply display pictures, a description, and the price of the product in your store. When someone orders the item and pays you, then you order from Oberlo, and they will pack and ship it directly to your customer. All you need to do is market your store and products! What a deal!

Facebook, Instagram, Pinterest, and **YouTube.** You can't just open a store or website and hope clients will find it. You've got to create a following and drive customers to your site. Some of the more successful sellers I have seen are social media personalities. They appear on Instagram, Facebook, and YouTube, doing fun things with their products. Fisherwomen appear on boats and with fish, wearing cute turtle necklaces and bracelets—then sell the heck out of them in their Etsy stores. Not because they placed an ad, but because of the way the photo made the customer *feel*. This is one of the most important marketing techniques to learn: make people *feel* free to *feel* the wind in their hair and the sun on their back, while visualizing themselves on a boat or a beach. No worries—they will buy lots of turtle bracelets!

Pictures of people on horses sell Western wear. People on surfboards sell rash guards and skins. People on skis sell winter wear. Find your niche, your passion, the thing to which you can bring uniqueness, and build a community around it. A community of like-minded people will consume products related to their common interests—fishing, shooting, team sports, cats, dogs, horses, boating, vegan culture, fitness, and many more. Do a little research online and build your niche.

One good strategy is use a cadence of subjects in Instagram photos. If you're selling jewelry, post two or three outdoor pictures with you or your family and then a lifestyle photo of one of your jewelry pieces. A lifestyle photo is different from a normal advertising photo. The images are interesting to follow; they're not just product pitches. Put the link to your website or store in your Instagram bio, because Instagram doesn't allow you to put links in each post.

Image building is similar on Facebook and YouTube. Images and videos are powerful communicators but need to be interesting. Seek to make an emotional or spiritual connection with your audience. People follow people on social media; they are less likely to follow companies or products. I may have the Chick-fil-A app on my phone, but I never go to their Instagram page (although I do follow their CEO, Dan Cathy, on social media).

If your business is service-related rather than product-related, you may want to use videos rather than images. After all, it's difficult to create interesting pictures of you doing virtual assistant work. Instead, your videos can be filled with interesting tips and information related to your niche. Videos on how to save time or get organized, if those subjects relate to your business, are great ways to build an audience. Post one video per week.

One favorite example, which I've already profiled, is Iguana Solutions in Florida, which has tons of social media posts, photos, and videos of them capturing invasive species. They're fun to watch.

I've also mentioned Gretchen Menard, who has turned the least glamorous job in the world into something that's fun to watch. You can find her series, "Riding Shotgun with Gretchen Menard," on YouTube. We get to ride along as she services her portable restroom business, and the best thing about it is that she is just being herself. Her genuineness comes through. Gretchen is creating authentic community engagement with her videos. The business name is unforgettable too—Poopy's Potties—and her video "Where Does the Poop Go?" is a classic. (Gretchen also operates Swanky Restrooms, profiled above.)

You may think I'm wacky because I find humor in these potentially unloved businesses, but it supports my thesis that you can build a million-dollar business from the simplest ideas and by meeting the most basic of customer needs. Anecdotally, all the portable restroom business owners I have met are millionaires, reinforcing this idea that you can excel in an uncomplicated or seemingly old-school business and build a thriving enterprise.

The process I typically use for managing Internet content and traffic is to post as much content as possible on my blog, which is on my website, then share the link for the blog post, with a teaser or introductory sentence or paragraph on Facebook, Instagram, Twitter, and LinkedIn. If I have an interesting article on how to do something, I post it first on the blog with a good image or video, then create a post on social media that includes an image or video, the first paragraph of the article, followed by a link that says, "To read more, click here." In order for viewers to read the article, they will click the link and finish reading the article or post on my blog. They are now on my website, which is where you want to drive your audience. On the sidebar and bottom of the article's page on your blog, you will put a call to action box or tool. If you sell a product, the call to action will be a link to your store. If you sell a service, this tool is a contact form to request more information (the prospect fills in their name and email) or an autodial button to your business phone number.

This is your flow: engage viewers on social media, attract them to your website or store, then convert them into customers: engagement, attraction, conversion.

Be sure to refer to my descriptions of content marketing and the call to action in the glossary at the back of this book.

Other companies that provide similar support to sellers are:

Spocket.co./Modalyst.co, who can give you access to top brands like Calvin Klein and Puma.

ProductPro avoids Asian suppliers and focuses on 50,000 US-based products.

UniteXpress.com helps you present and edit your products as well as create pricing.

Importify.com is an app that allows you to access multiple suppliers and aggregate them to your site.

Spreadr.co allows you to either drop-ship or affiliate with them, linking you to Amazon so you can add their goods to your store in order to make it look bigger; then you can earn a commission on sales.

Shipstation.com doesn't provide drop-shipping of your merchandise, but it helps you compare shipping rates, print shipping labels, and track shipments. They also provide a shipment tracking tool for customers, which you can plug into your website.

20

Selling Your Services

*Approach each customer with the idea of helping him or her to solve
a problem or achieve a goal, not of selling a product or service.*
—BRIAN TRACY, MOTIVATIONAL SPEAKER

Selling traditional services online will require you to have your
own website as well as a processing system on your site that can
accept payments for your services. If you don't use a third party
such as Upwork or Fiverr (which I'll discuss below), you will need
to build e-commerce into your website.

You will first need an SSL certificate to prove your site is secure.
You should be able to add that on with your hosting plan. Secondly,
you will need a merchant account to process credit cards.

MerchantOneProcessing.com is one of the lowest priced, beginning at only 0.29 percent of your transactions for retail or online.

Square.com/us/en is popular but also charges some of the highest
fees, beginning around 3.35 percent + 15 cents per transaction.

PayPal is another option, at around 1.5 percent, but not everyone
has a PayPal account. Buyers are sometimes confused because they

don't realize they can pay through your PayPal system with a credit card.

QuickBooks. Many people I know use payment processing from within their cloud-based QuickBooks accounting programs. It is superconvenient but carries fees that range from 1 percent for ACH (direct bank-to-bank payments) to 3.4 percent for keyed transactions.

Venmo and **Zelle** are also options for receiving and sending money. No fees involved.

Virtual Marketplaces for Services That Offer Payment Processing

If your virtual or home-based business includes an online deliverable such as those listed in this book, like those for virtual assistants, transcriptionists, graphics and design, website design, digital marketing, writing and translation, video and animation, music and audio, or programming and tech support, you may want to list yourself on **UpWork** or **Fiverr**. They not only connect customers with freelancers but process payments for you as well.

Fiverr.com is a marketplace for experts and freelancers that provides a one-stop solution for customers seeking services in 120 categories, according to the company.

Freelancer.com claims to have 30 million users and allows customers to post jobs to which freelancers will respond.

UpWork.com is a marketplace similar to Freelancer, where the customer will provide a job description, sometimes collateral material (such as a recording to transcribe), and a desired price, price range, budget, or price ceiling. Freelancers will respond or bid on the job. The customer will choose the best fit, make a down payment or put money in escrow toward a milestone, then make final payment when the work is complete. Upwork handles all the payment processing between the parties.

Use these tools, resources, websites, and online partners to start your business quickly and move rapidly to success. The new digital marketplace is telling us where the scarcity is and where the demand for value is—it's *you*! These amazing digital resources are ubiquitous, and they're everywhere, easy to access, and nearly free, which means the missing ingredient is *you*. The global marketplace needs people like you, with ideas and vision and who are willing to work hard and grow a business. E-commerce companies are rolling out the red carpet, saying, "Come on into the gig economy; we need you. We've built your store or marketplace for you. We just need your uniqueness, ingenuity, and hard work."

This is the best economy in history. There's never been a better time to be an entrepreneur. Get out there and seize the day!

21

Get Started!

Now that I've given you some tools and raw materials, I hope you'll start building your dream business. Think it through, write it down, but don't delay. Procrastination is the graveyard of dreams. Set the goal, write down your vision for the business (your value story) in one sentence, identify one or two key initiatives, and get started today.

Procrastination is the graveyard of dreams.

This opportunity is for everyone, everywhere. We all long for the dignity of financial independence. Beneath the struggle to provide food and shelter for our families, to pay our bills and to make ends meet, there is an aching desire for financial freedom and self-reliance. While gifts and charity can temporarily relieve economic lack, the only way to truly end financial challenges and the hopelessness that sometimes accompanies it is to empower and equip people to find and build better lives, economic independence, and security for themselves.

With this book, I want to empower, equip, and teach you to be free. I want you to be cured of the "not enough money" virus. I want you to be free from economic chains, dependence upon others, and the prison of debt. Free from building someone else's dream. If you embrace the inspiration of the stories in this book and act on some of my suggestions, you will earn your freedom and fulfill the purpose for which you were created: to honor God, to "go confidently in the direction of your dreams," and "live the life you've imagined," as Thoreau wrote.

Imagine a five-foot-tall man who has fallen into an eight-foot deep hole. He looks up and sees the top. His way of escape and freedom is just inches beyond his fingertips. He tries to jump out of his hole but finds that he cannot jump high enough to reach the edge. If only he could get a hand on that edge, he would find a way to pull himself out.

"I'll climb out," he thinks. So he begins clawing at the side of his hole but immediately finds that the side is loose and crumbling. The more he claws at it, the more it falls in on him.

Do you ever feel as if you are in a hole? That your money life is like a hole from which you cannot escape? You see the way out, you jump, and you stretch, but cannot quite reach it. You scrape and claw and work at it, but it just keeps falling in on you.

I could drop some food to you in your hole, but you would still be in your hole. Instead, what I want to do in this book is to empower you to be ten feet tall. You are going to grow your way out of your hole. If you grow tall and strong, you will never have to worry about falling into the money pit again. You will have grown your way out. You are going to grow intellectually and spiritually and build a strong and quiet depth of character.

I want to make you a giant. Through these chapters, we've planted the seeds together—the seeds of the eternal principles, ethics, and techniques that will empower you to be ten feet tall, not physically, but spiritually big, intellectually strong, and having an ethical spine of steel. In this way you will grow your way to financial independence.

A Formula for Hope

Freedom has spread rapidly throughout the world. Nonetheless, challenges remain. The news is full of stories about economic inequality, racism, and political repression around the world. While political solutions and activism have their place, I want to give you the proven formula for hope. Be the light in the darkness. Be a good man or woman; serve your family and your community. Your family will thrive, your business will thrive, your community will thrive, and you will be changing the world. Be the candle in the darkness. Embrace the opportunity and promise of the future, and go forth to do great good works.

In developing countries, there are challenges for entrepreneurs and families that may be different than those in developed countries with more mature economies. In parts of one country, you may not have easy access to goods and supplies, in another, you may not have the full security and protection of the rule of law, and in another, you may have a less educated labor pool. However, these challenges are actually ingredients in the formula of hope. Your potential rate of growth is greater in a challenged or difficult community or in an emerging or developing economy than it is in a developed economy. I believe that the degree by which you can improve your life is greater in Kampala than in London. Did you know that the GDP (gross domestic product) growth rate is greater in Uganda than it is in the United States?

In Uganda, you can achieve a good standard of living by improving your income from a $3 to $11 per day. This is a threefold increase. By contrast, a Londoner would starve on an income of $11 a day. Everything is relative to the social and economic structure in your community. Just make sure you are climbing the ladder and not sitting on a rung with your face in your hands, crying that the world has not brought you success and fortune. Stand up and start climbing.

They Don't Know You Yet, But They Love You

There is hope and there is help. If you read nothing else, I've written I want you to read this, know this, memorize this—there is no such thing as hopelessness, no dead end, no loneliness. There is always hope, there is always a way of escape, and amazingly there are these people in your community that may not even know you but they love you, they've been praying for you, and they will do anything to help you succeed, to escape the life of want and despair. You'll find them waiting for you at church, at the mission, at the prison literacy program. They love you, and they will help you—not with cash, but with support, education, or a fast start for your new life or business.

Even as I'm writing this, I'm thinking about some of the toughest places to start a business and live a God-honoring life. El Salvador, which is rife with gangs, Pakistan with its cultural crosscurrents, remote Mongolia, war-torn Syria and Burma are all such places. But you know what? I have friends in each of those places. They are there, helping teach and lift people up in those challenging communities.

Never let your situation or circumstances keep you from turning to God and beginning your journey to freedom. The formula for hope works everywhere, all the time, and for everyone.

You may be thinking, "I'm not poor or lacking hope. I'm middle-class, and I just want to start a business." So join me in helping others. Feel empathy for those less fortunate than you. As you succeed in life and business, be sure you're always extending a hand to help someone up. You can be a mentor or encourager. You'll be doing what you were made for!

For those that want help outside developed economies, people like our friends at World Challenge's Poverty Solutions are ready and willing to come alongside you. They'll help you discover your strength, find your dream, and learn how to grow yourself into the place you want to be.

This book is intended to be a tool for people in almost any culture, a quiver of idea-arrows that hopeful entrepreneurs can shoot flaming toward their dreams.

Go at it boldly, and you'll find unexpected forces closing round you and coming to your aid.   —Basil King

---

The Man or Woman in the Mirror

Look in the mirror. What do you see? Is it a good person, or . . . ? Who are you today, and who or what do you want to be three years from now? That person in the mirror is the key to your destiny, a blessed family, and business success. Great businesses are built on people and a good culture. Perhaps you will see the launch of your business as both a natural and spiritual journey, as I do. If you commit yourself to honesty, integrity, listening to others, and serving people, you will succeed. You'll be changing your life and the lives of those in your circle at the same time.

Money is only a tool. It will take you wherever you wish, but it will not replace you as the driver.   —Ayn Rand

---

Making money is not the goal of life, or of this book. Making money is easy, but our goal is to live a life that honors God and helps others. I want you to build on this foundation and live a life that provides financial and physical security for your family as well as enough abundance to help others. If you put all your focus on the acquisition of money, you won't succeed; in the end, you'll fail to hang on to the money, and you'll miss the real purpose of life, for which money is just a tool. I have watched many entrepreneurs succeed in business, make a lot of money, then fall into the predictable cycle of using their newfound wealth to abuse drugs and alcohol and indulge the spirit of envy and covetousness with houses, cars, boats, jewelry, and materialistic obsessions. In a few years they end up dead or dead broke.

Instead, put God first, then others, then yourself. Live by this axiom, and you will find success not only with money, but with your whole life.

At the end of the day, it's not about what you have or even what you've accomplished. It's about who you've lifted up. Who you've made better. It's about what you've given back.   —Denzel Washington

---

22

Glossary

Brand. According to the American Marketing Association (AMA), a brand is a name, term, design, symbol or any other feature that identifies one seller's good or service as distinct from those of other sellers. ISO (International Organization for Standardization) brand standards add that a brand "is an intangible asset" that is intended to create "distinctive images and associations in the minds of stakeholders, thereby generating economic benefit/values."

Brand promise. The experience your customer will receive each time they interact with your company. It is more than the product or service, because it includes the quality and consistency of the entire customer experience or customer journey (see "Customer experience" below) from discovery to the decision to buy to the delivery. The more you can deliver that experience, product, and service consistently, the stronger your brand will be in your customers' mind.

Cloud. The cloud, or cloud-based computing, is a network of remote servers (computers) accessed through the Internet that manage, store, and process data and programs in lieu of personal computers or local servers (such as one housed in your office). Users usually rent space on these servers or pay subscription fees to use the programs.

Content marketing. A form of marketing by which you create and share interesting, helpful, educational, or entertaining material such as social media posts, articles, blogs, and videos that are not specifically promoting your product or service but are intended to inform, entertain, which will ultimately stimulate interest in your service or product. It may establish you as subject matter expert related to a service or inspire people to make an emotional connection to your mission or product.

Customer experience. Often referred to as the *CX*, this is the customer's journey from seeking a product or service to the end of the road, where they receive and use it. Your job is to understand the customer's experience from their perspective. Is it convenient, simple, elegant, enjoyable, fun, and efficient? Does the customer reach the end of the journey saying they are ecstatic, happy, and in love with you, your product, or your service? You should track the metrics of your customer engagement so you know how you're doing. Get feedback. Aim to go past customer satisfaction to customer delight.

Customer journey. Your customer's complete experience with your organization. It spans all of the customer's interactions across all departments, devices, and touchpoints throughout each phase of the customer life cycle—from the initial awareness of your brand to prospect to customer to long-term loyalty.

Differentiator. The business attribute(s) and/or unique value that clearly separate your product or service from the competition in a particular marketplace. A key differentiator should be unique, measurable, and defendable, according to SmartMarketingLLC.com.

Due diligence. The reasonable steps you should take in order to satisfy a requirement of adequate care, especially related to buying or selling something. It is often in the form of a comprehensive appraisal of a business that is done by the prospective buyer, especially to establish its true assets, liabilities, and commercial potential. One key activity of due diligence is to verify that the claims of the seller are true and verifiable and can be documented or validated, often with the help of third parties (such as accountants, appraisers, and attorneys). A manufacturer may claim that they will provide you with great service or support, but customers or third-party rating agencies may tell you a different story. If you are buying a company, they may claim they are making $1 million, but their records may only show $800,000.

Emerging affluent. A demographic defined as households and individuals with household incomes over $125,000 and over $100,000 in liquid financial assets.

High-net-worth (HNW) or high-net-worth individual (HNWI). A demographic defined as including those with at least $1 million in cash or liquid assets, excluding the value of their homes.

Lifestyle photos. Lifestyle photography creates images of people in real life settings and activities "in an artistic manner and the art of the everyday" (Wikipedia). In marketing, lifestyle images and videos inspire people to feel a certain way about a product or service. They let people's lives tell the story of a product or company's story rather than simply advertising or offering products and services.

Marketing. According to the American Marketing Association (AMA), the activity, set of institutions, and processes for creating, communicating, delivering, and exchanging offerings that have value for customers, clients, partners, and society at large.

Market saturation. This happens when the volume of a product or service in the marketplace has been maximized. Regarding the theory of natural limits, economist Thomas G. Osenton states, "Every product or service has a natural consumption level. We just don't know what it is until we launch it, distribute it, and promote it for a generation's time (20 years or more) after which further investment to expand the universe beyond normal limits can be a futile exercise."

Mass-affluent. A demographic at the upper end of the mass market. Households or individuals with $100,000 up to $1 million in liquid assets and an income over $75,000 are considered mass- affluent.

Remote work. An arrangement by which employees work away from the company and use digital tools to communicate, including email, telephone, video conferencing, and collaboration platforms such as Salesforce, Slack, and Skype. Management and collaboration techniques and resources are evolving rapidly to accommodate the popularity (and sometimes necessity) of remote work.

ROI, or return on investment. How you measure the amount of return on an investment based on its cost. If you earn net $10,000 on $100,000 investment in a building, your ROI is 10 percent.

Ultra-high-net-worth (UHNW). A demographic identifying people whose net worth is $30 million or more.

Very-high-net-worth (VHNW). A demographic that describes people with more than $5 million in cash or liquid assets, excluding their primary residence.

White-label products and advertising. A product, website, or catalog that is created by one party, such as a manufacturer, but rebranded to make it appear it belongs to another party, often the retailer. Manufacturers, wholesalers, distributors, and affinity groups often create products and marketing tools that sellers can brand as their own. This helps both parties sell more.

X-factor. A special or noteworthy variable or quality that is more than a differentiator (see "differentiator" above) and makes an emotional or spiritual connection with customers or potential customers and influences their decision to buy from you.

22

A Mini–Business Plan

Academics recommend several formats and methods for business plans, which range from simple to very complex. Below I am setting out a mini–business plan to get you started on your new endeavor. I want to give you an outline for beginning; it may be all you need, or you may want to expand it into a much more detailed plan, depending on the complexity of your business. You decide how much time and detail you want to put into this plan.

My Story

1. What is my story—my value proposition?

_____

_____

_____

2. How am I unique? How will my business stand out in the crowd of other businesses?

_____

_____

_____

3. What customer problem am I solving, or whose need am I satisfying?

_____

_____

_____

Who?

1. Who are my ideal clients?

Example: Busy professionals who prefer that service providers
come to them rather than having to drive to a business.

Example: People with disposable income, such as mass affluent,
high net worth (HNW), and ultra high net worth (UHNW) individuals.

_____

_____

_____

2. Why will they buy from me?

_____

_____

_____

What?

1. What are you selling? A product, a service, or both?

_____

_____

_____

Example: products: cleansers, creams, and treatments

Example: a service: haircuts

Example: both: manicure and polish

Efficacy

Does my product or service solve a problem or meet a need? Is it appealing, desirable, and/or in demand?

How?

1. How will I deliver my products or services?

_____

_____

_____

2. Is my product digital? Or does it require door-to-door delivery?

_____

_____

_____

Partners

1. Who are my suppliers and distributors?

_____

_____

_____

2. Whom do I need to partner with to ensure my success?

_____

_____

_____

3. Whom will I do business with to ensure my success (subcontractors and strategic alliances, such as graphic designers and wholesalers)?

_____

_____

_____

Spread the Love

Building deep, lasting customer relationships. (These are often called business development activities.)

  1. How do I acquire, attract, keep, and grow customers?

_____

_____

_____

  2. How will I build a loyal following?

_____

_____

_____

Resources and Inventory

  1. What do I bring to the game?

_____

_____

_____

  2. What do I need to make the business work—monetary, physical, intellectual, or human capital?

_____

_____

_____

Money In (Revenue)

  1. What is my expected income?

_____

_____

_____

2. What do I need to make a good living and make a profit?

_____

_____

_____

Money Out (Overhead and Costs)

1. What are my fixed monthly costs (rent, lease, etc.)?

_____

_____

_____

2. What are my variable monthly costs (supplies, utilities, etc.)?

_____

_____

_____

About the Author

Only by helping others succeed
do we succeed ourselves.
—JIM PALUMBO

Jim Palumbo has started more than a dozen companies and advised business owners for over thirty years. He knows how to build businesses from thin air, without money or advanced training, and teaches entrepreneurs how to succeed in the small business world while leading meaningful lives.

Jim is the president of World Radio Network and founder and president of EvangAlliance, Inc., a nonprofit that is taking the message of hope to those that need it most. He is a principal at Dynamic Advisor Solutions, providing consulting, support, and business systems to successful wealth advisors who want to elevate their practices.

Jim developed his love of teaching as a professor at Logos University and a pastor in New York City. He is a founding member of Times Square Church and serves on the boards of various nonprofit organizations.

Jim says the thing he enjoys most is being husband to Cheri and Dad to Gia and Jordan. This is followed by a love for fly-fishing, which he enjoys in the Rocky Mountains, near his home in Colorado Springs, or at his home away from home on the Texas Gulf Coast.

www.JimPalumbo.com